WHEN HOPE FOUND ME

Stories of Inspiration, Triumph, and Hope

Kim Lengling

Lead Author: Kim Lengling

Book Cover Design: Kim Lengling

Stock photo(s)-Canva

Proof-readers: Ruth L. Anderson, Kim Lengling, Sandra Pottorf

Editor: Ruth L. Anderson

Publisher: Kim Lengling

Printed in the United States of America

First Printing Edition, 2022

ISBN: 978-1-0881-4570-8

Table of Contents

The Ripple Effect

When you throw a pebble into a pond, you will see a splash and hear the resounding plunk of the pebble.

You may notice concentric circles rippling from where the pebble hit the water.

It is the hope that this book will act as a pebble being tossed into the water, creating ripples that will gently flow and reach just who they are meant to reach.

"I alone cannot change the world, but I can cast a stone across the waters to create many ripples."

– MOTHER TERESA

INTRODUCTION

When Hope Found Me is an anthology. What is an anthology, exactly? According to Dictionary.com, the explanation is a book or other collection of selected writings by various authors, usually in the same literary form, of the same period, or on the same subject.

The subject of the stories within this book are stories of hope.

Have you ever felt hopeless? A traumatic event in your life, the loss of a loved one, a job, or a divorce.

All those things and more can bring you a feeling of hopelessness. But then something happens. A person reaches out to you. You receive an email or a card from someone saying they are thinking of you. It could be a song you hear on the radio or a show you have watched on television. Perhaps it is in your pet's eyes as they come up to snuggle against you. Maybe it is a connection with a stranger in line at the grocery store.

Hope. It is everywhere if your eyes and heart are open to receiving it. God works things out in His time and in His way.

I pray the stories in this book will provide a nugget of hope for you; that there will be one story that touches you in a way that makes you think, "Ah…ok, I'm not the only one. I CAN get through this."

Each co-author has shared a personal part of their life, hoping it will touch someone and provide that small spark of light.

We all have a light within us. It may sometimes dim, but don't you dare let it go out! The world needs your light. The world needs you!

Once your light is burning a bit brighter, share it with others. Be that small breath of air that fans the flame for someone else.

The world can be a dark place. My prayers and hopes are that this book is a light for those sitting in a dark place.

A light that provides a glimmer of hope can turn into a burning flame.

Shine on, dear ones. The world needs your light!

Kim Lengling

Dr. Skip Mondragon

"He hath shewed thee, O, man, what is good: and what doth the LORD require of thee, but to do justly, and to love mercy, and to walk humbly with thy God."

(MICAH 6:8, KJV)

Twenty-six-year Army veteran, and retired Colonel, Dr. Skip Mondragon has spoken to tough guys struggling with depression since 2014. He became a casualty of depression during his last year in the Army.

During his recovery, he was called to help other men. Skip is a National Wrestling Champion, the author of the award-winning book Wrestling is Not for Wimps, a TEDx speaker, and has been married to Sherry for 41 years.

FORWARD

I met Kim through her podcast Let Fear Bounce. We had an instant connection. We are fellow veterans, speakers, and authors. Yet, a deeper chord was struck. We had both suffered deeply. Our wounds were grievous. Out of our deep suffering, we found healing, a renewed purpose, and relentless determination to serve others. Our messes became our messages. My respect for her has grown as we have interacted since September 2021.

She has shared her story of betrayal and sexual assault while serving on active duty in the military with raw emotion and honesty. As a retired Army Colonel, hearing stories like Kim's, I become enraged. As fellow service members, we are committed to honor, protect, and, if need be, lay our lives down for each other. I cannot think of a more personal and horrendous breach of that commitment. Over time, Kim climbed out of the pit of darkness and despair to build a new life.

She is an ambassador of hope. My sister in service to others and in Christ, has not slowed her pace. She's contributed to more books, spoken on larger stages, hosts a TV program, and shows no signs of slowing down. Oh, did I forget to mention Kim is a dedicated member at her local veterans' post, the Veterans of the Vietnam War (VVnW, Post 52), where she spreads her joy and hope and has been dubbed "the kid"?

You do not have to be around this lady long to appreciate her joy and gratitude. It is infectious. She approaches life with gusto. Yet, despite all her accomplishments and accolades, she remains humble and down-to-earth.

Kim's message and the stories shared in this book will inspire you not to give up in the face of suffering. They will give you hope amid your darkest days. And they will give you the courage to know that you are not alone.

I am honored to count Kim as my sister and fellow overcomer. You will do well to listen to her.

Donald G. "Skip" Mondragon, MD, MPH
Colonel, U.S. Army, Retired

KIM LENGLING

"You will be secure, because there is hope; you will look about you and take your rest in safety"

(JOB 11:18, NIV)

Through a Dog's Eyes

Can you find hope in a dog? My answer would be an unequivocal yes.

I have been a dog lover my entire life. I have always had a dog. Their pure souls and unconditional love should not be taken for granted. Think about it. They spend their entire life waiting on their human to spend time with them. That is a lot of waiting if you work full-time, have kids, etc.

I have loved each dog that has been a part of my life. But there is one I will talk about, think about, and still tear up over for the rest of my life.

His name was Digger. A Black Lab/Shepherd mix and one of the most intelligent dogs I have ever known. You could tell him something once, and he learned it immediately. He was protective, watchful, and oh-so caring.

Digger was a rescue. I rescued him at 13 weeks old at our local Shelter. He had a goofy little face, big floppy ears, and a tail with a poof of fur on the tip. He was unique, and I knew he would become a part of our family.

At his adoption, I did not foresee my future; being divorced, having my daughter grow up and moving out on her own, and my health turning.

It seemed as if it was just Digger and me all at once. We came up with our own mutual routine and way of living. Daily walks, without fail, in whatever weather. Snuggles. Yard work, shoveling snow, and in all manner of things, Digger was by my side "helping."

As our bond grew even closer when it was just the two of us living together, I realized that Digger could sense things with me, even before I could.

You see, I live with PTSD due to experiencing military sexual assault. PTSD is different for everyone. Anxiety and depression play a big part in my life. More so at certain times of the year.

I noticed that Digger would stick close to me at certain times. He would lean his 105-pound body against mine or nudge me with his nose. He would be sure to lay in the doorway of whatever room I was in as if to keep me in his sight. If we were in public, he would occasionally place his body directly in front of mine as if creating a barrier.

I realized his actions would notch up when I was having a difficult day. When I say difficult day, I mean no restful sleep; I would be anxious or "edgy," as I like to say. In addition, my jaw would be sore from clenching it throughout the day or night while I slept.

Digger would notice and took it upon himself to take care of me. Oh, the tears that fell onto his fur, the hugs he endured, and the quiet times he stayed by my side.

Unconditional love and care from my beautiful Digger gave me hope to get through a tough day, see the world through his eyes, and see the beauty in the small things.

We took walks twice a day, and at times, he was my sole motivation for heading out. We had to go for our walks. My life revolved around him and his needs, and his life revolved around protecting and caring for his human Mum.

I began to write short stories of what conversations between him and me would be like. For years I wrote little stories and began sharing them on social media. Silly chats about what Digger may be thinking or how he may be teaching his Mum something. There were always little lessons to the conversations; some were funny, and some were quite deep at times.

I realized those stories were something people began to look forward to. People would comment on how bright Digger was or how his Mum was lucky to have such a wise dog.

I shared everything that happened in our lives, or our Realm, as I began to call it: Digger, The Mighty Black Dog, The Keeper of The Watch, and his Mum.

The stories "we" shared began to resonate with the people reading them. I would get questions from strangers and people I knew who wanted to know what Digger would be up to next. It was as if people forgot that it was a human writing the stories, not a dog.

I realized those stories brought little sparks of joy and hope to people who were on the journey of life with Digger and me.

As with all dogs, their lives are too short. But the last years of Digger's life were filled with what his entire life had been filled with - love, adventures, walks, and sharing stories.

As he aged, he became slower and a bit more tired. His stories changed a bit as well. He began to get philosophical with his stories. Talking to the other critters within his Realm to be sure his Mum would be okay when he would no longer be around to care for her.

He knew it would be hard for his Mum, but he also knew his job was to be sure he did what he could to ensure she was okay.

As for me? Digger's Mum? I knew the time was coming and prepared myself the best that I could. Digger was still teaching me lessons; only now, they were more about patience, kindness, and hope.

Diggers' final year was bittersweet and filled with so much love. Even when his body slowed down, he still had that spark in his eyes. He stayed by my side or in the doorway of whatever room I was in. He still wanted his twice daily walks, even though they became shorter and shorter.

I prayed and hoped that his passing would be gentle, and it was. I prayed that he would be healthy and happy in heaven. I had a dream three weeks after he died that showed me, he was. I prayed and hoped that I was enough for him, that I gave him all the love I could, and was assured by God that I had.

Oh, the hurt. I cannot describe it. For me, it was crushing because it is NEVER just a dog. Digger was a massive part of my life and healing and will forever be part of my heart.

Hope. Digger gave me hope when I felt lost. I know that God sent him. That perfect dog for a hurting soul.

And then God sent another dog into my life, even when I was determined not to open my heart to future potential hurt. Five months after I said goodbye to Digger, I felt a whisper while driving to work. "There is a dog that needs you." I immediately replied, "No, God. I can't do it."

God is God, and He repeated, "There is a dog that needs you." Well, I found myself on the local shelter's website. Only one dog was listed on the site, which is unusual. So, I called and made an appointment to visit after work.

That evening, I found myself sitting on the floor of the shelter's "get acquainted " room as they brought in this skinny, ill, and skittish dog. He had a fawn-colored body, a black head, white toes, one blue eye, and one brown eye. So different from Digger.

I said nothing. I figured this dog had to pick me if this was meant to be. I sat, waiting him out. He would inch closer, sniff my hand, and back away. This went on for a while. Still, I said nothing. I sat on the floor until, eventually, this fearful dog came to my side, leaned his body against mine, and placed his chin on my shoulder with that one ice-blue eye staring up at me. It was at that point I whispered, "Oh my…I think you're coming home with me, aren't you?"

Hope. Hope is what I saw in that bright blue eye staring up at me. Hope for a home and love. And dare I say, a bit of hope began to fill my heart again.

God provides hope where he sees fit and in the most unexpected places.

Hope found me in the eyes of an ill, skittish dog at the local shelter who has since filled my life with laughter and new eyes with which to see the world. A world filled with hope.

He has also started sharing stories of his life with his "Lady Mum," as he calls her. They are different stories from Diggers. The stories are shared with a younger perspective and are often silly. But he is tossing nuggets of light in his unique way, little nuggets of hope to an often, too dark world.

Thank you, God, for nudging me yet again.

ANNETTE RUTH PEARSON

"You go before me and follow me. You place your hand of blessing on my head. Such knowledge is too wonderful for me, too great for me to understand!"

(PSALM 139: 5-6, NLT)

Hope in the Middle of Loss

The last couple of years has been tough for me emotionally, like most individuals worldwide. Certain events have rocked me to the core and left a dark cloud over myself and others. Yet, at other times it feels like you are swimming in water, and instead of coming to the surface for air, you go deeper and deeper to the bottom.

When you are a child and see adults around you – parents and grandparents- you never imagine you will occupy their positions one day. A time will come when they will be laid to rest, and the cycle of life will continue. But then you grow up, and you attend their funerals, and you have the hope one day you will be reunited with them.

At each of their funerals, those in attendance were reminded of the promise Jesus gave His disciples as He faced the reality of His own death, John 14: 1-3, NLT.

"Don't let your hearts be troubled. Trust in God, and trust also in me. There is more than enough room in my Father's home. If this were not so, would I have told you that I am going to prepare a place for you? When everything is ready, I will come and get you so that you will always be with me where I am."

But how do you cope with the loss of your peers, not one but three, within a brief period? How do you manage when you thought God would heal a person as He had done in the past? This reflection is about the first of these losses.

I remember the Saturday morning we learned that my friend had only a few days to live unless God performed a miracle. The news was difficult to take in, as I also thought about their family, my adopted family, which would be left behind. I sent a voice message with a prayer and words of encouragement.

My church decided to hold a 24-hour prayer vigil for the family, praying together at set times as a church community starting that night. Different members of the church would prepare something to share for each prayer session. As we sat in one of the sessions, we realized there was a call from the hospital for the pastor and his wife to attend, yet we were still hopeful. God heard our prayers, and we were able to complete the vigil. We were still hopeful that God would turn things around.

On Wednesday evening, during a prayer meeting, we were all informed of positive progress that day. Hope had revived again.

So, you can imagine the disbelief when the call came to say he had died the following morning. It was hard to take in the words. My mind would not accept them.

Others became concerned about my health and how my body would respond to the news, as we were very close. Our love was as strong as biological siblings, or even stronger. Would I have a lupus flare-up as I had in the past? Would my body be able to cope with this news?

God was faithful to His promise that the healing that had taken place in my body years ago would be permanent. This news would not put me back into a hospital bed. But it was difficult, extremely difficult.

I remember the first time going to visit the family, and we held each other in our arms and cried. We did not have to share words; the embrace said it all. As I write this now, emotions still flood back, but now there is an unusual peace instead of pain. The peace that only God can give.

The peace which is found in John 14:27, NLT

"I am leaving you with a gift—peace of mind and heart. And the peace I give is a gift the world cannot give. So don't be troubled or afraid."

This peace truly is a gift as it is not something you can obtain yourself. It is a spiritual gift, and it takes time to fully appreciate your peace of mind and heart. It is a double gift because God knew and knows you need both – peace in your mind and peace in your heart.

Peace in your mind as you go on an emotional journey. The journey can feel as if you are walking down a hill into a dark valley, and as you walk, you wonder when you will reach the bottom. As your walk continues, you go through the emotions of denial, fear, and anger, to name a few. If you have been on this journey, you can understand.

Eventually, you reach the stage of acceptance and realize that you need to rebuild your life with the people you love not being with you physically, but you still have their memories. When planning events, you can indirectly include them in what they would say or do if they were still with you.

Acceptance is the turning point. You begin to walk back up the other side of that hill, and as you walk, you can see the light at the top, but it is not easy to walk up.

Sometimes you want to go back down as it is easier to walk down than up, but you know that in the valley, life does not function the way you would like, so you climb one step at a time. As you look around, you see others rising with you, making the journey easier as you can share your feelings and emotions and realize you are not alone. Others are feeling the pain of loss and separation too. You are comforted and now understand the gift of peace of mind and heart.

At the time of writing, I have not been able to visit their resting place, despite having opportunities to go. In my mind, they are on an extended holiday, and one day they will return, but I know that is not the case. I believe we will see each other on the day Jesus spoke about when He would return and take all His children home to occupy the mansions His Father is preparing for us.

Where am I now in this loss process?

God has a way of getting our attention if we are still enough.

In the quietness of the night, He sees the tears that fall from your eyes and collects them into a bottle, as He promised us in His words, as found in Psalm 56:8, NLT.

"You keep track of all my sorrows. You have collected all my tears in your bottle. You have recorded each one in your book."

In the quietness of the night, when you cannot sleep, He speaks words of reassurance if you open your ears to listen to His voice.

I was preparing a sermon based on Psalm 139. I have always liked this Psalm as it reminds me that I am fearfully and wonderfully made. It reminds me that God has a plan for my life; no matter what I go through, He is always there. As I was delivering the sermon, the Holy Spirit spoke with me and told me to call a friend to illustrate the verse I have chosen as my special one for this reading,

"You go before me and follow me.
    You place your hand of blessing on my head.
  Such knowledge is too wonderful for me,
    too great for me to understand!"

In the illustration, I needed to go and stand in front of my friend. I was before them. Then I needed to stand behind them as if I were following them. Then I needed to stand at their side and place my hand of blessing on their head.

I had a lightbulb moment.

God was showing me and all of us who were in the church, He has gone before us. Everything which has happened, He was us. He is following us, so He has made provision for what may come. But today, this very moment, He has His hand of blessing on my head. What I am going through may not feel like a blessing, but God is with me as I walk.

As a church family, we have grown stronger, and there is more love and togetherness. The journey has not been easy, but I can now find hope amid loss.

MESHELL BAKER

"The person who does not clearly declare their future will be
defined by their past."

Life Without Purpose is a Prison

Okay, where do I begin? I could start by telling you one of my first memories of childhood was the harsh reality that I was a mistake at birth, the result of an unplanned pregnancy, and an unwanted marriage born to two teenage parents. Or I could share that I owned three businesses by thirteen: babysitting, sewing/tailoring, and baking cookies and cakes. But by seventeen, my brilliance had been dimmed by life's hardships and multiple abusers, which led to barely graduating from high school. Yet, at nineteen, I sparked again, becoming the youngest management trainee at an electronics retailer branch. Here is when I made a life-altering mistake. I was young, insecure, and easily influenced. The guy I was dating convinced me that credit card fraud was harmless. I ended up arrested, convicted, and incarcerated at twenty years old.

After serving a minimal sentence thanks to a glowing recommendation from my youth pastor submitted to the judge, I found work. As you may imagine, there are few opportunities for a newly released convict. But, because I was determined never to return to prison, I took and did whatever job I could get. I decided to stay busy. I intended to do whatever it took, no matter what, to keep out of jail, and I did. Here is somewhere I can excel. I was an excellent worker, a supervisor's dream. This knack for being beneficial to the boss opened doors.

Around the age of twenty-five, I realized that working and partying were not enough. I began to want more. I set my sights on believing I could achieve, what looked like to me, the impossible. I wanted to be a boss, not just a worker, and I set about getting an education. I believed getting a college degree, and a professional job was the answer. It had to be. Everyone I saw who had college degrees seemed to be thriving. They were graduating, accepting great jobs, getting married, buying houses and cars, and OMG… starting families. That had to be it. It had to be how I finally found my amazing life right?

I applied to the local Community College and began my studies. I did well but struggled to keep up with my friends and my new dream, so I applied to a university in another state. Nothing like a fresh start. Accepted to Howard University, I packed up, set off to create my dream, and prevailed. I returned home in May of 1994 with a Bachelor of Business Administration and an entry-level job at a Fortune 500 company. I had graduated and secured an excellent job. Marriage and baby carriage would certainly be forthcoming.

Unfortunately, no. What I discovered was a cycle of self-destruction. An endless sense of doom and dread that I could not voice. I would create amazing opportunities and almost immediately shrink from fear. What if I wasn't ready? What if I wasn't enough? What if I failed and looked stupid? Seriously the fear, doubt, and second-guessing became so loud and redundant that I began to dial down my dreams. I began to believe that it wouldn't be hard to succeed if I wanted less. If I lowered my standards, I could meet someone. If I settled, I'd finally be happy. None of this is ever true for me or anyone.

Years passed with job and career success but no lasting relationship. Try as I might, my mate picker was off. I felt broken. I constantly asked myself, "What is wrong with me?" Which meant the dream of marriage, home, and baby carriage continued to be delayed. Yet hope prevailed as I continued to trust, "All things are possible for those who believe." I did finally meet someone, and my dream was reignited. I met my best friend and mate. But still, it was not to be. After seven years, the love of my life became ill and died. No marriage and no babies.

It wasn't until 18 months later, in March of 2012, that I reached my breaking point. I sat sad and depressed on my living room sofa. I was alone and underwhelmed by my so-called life staring at a bottle of aspirin. Wondering why. Really?! It had been eighteen years since declaring my intentions. All I had to show was a deceased fiancé, a job for which I was undertrained and ill-equipped, and a boss who was off the spectrum Bipolar, all while living in a city where I knew not one soul (no friends, no family in sight). Where was my prince charming and fairy tale life? And why is living so damn hard?!

Where I found myself that dark day in March 2012 turned out it was not a bad place. Yes, it felt bad. I mean bad. That was the worse emotional pain I have experienced in my life. But what I discovered was my resolve and willingness to live and live life more fully. I desired to become someone who never again got derailed by her circumstances. Situations and people gave birth to a purpose that became my guiding principle. I decided, determined, and declared my quest, and my self-discovery began.

I realized I had spent 20+ years chasing stuff and status because I thought it would make me happy. When I stopped chasing and looked around, I discovered happiness was an illusion. What I observed was name-calling, gossiping, rumor-spreading, competing, and comparing. So, I pressed pause and set out to discover my WHY. I stopped chasing people's approval and started choosing purposeful abundance. What I rediscovered was my original joy of being a valuable gift and sharing my joy.

This is where in the movies, everything ends happily ever after. I find my bliss and dismiss my blah. The reality is I've spent years on various quests of some sort. Always endeavoring to become better and create something amazing. So here I am twenty-odd years later, and what had I learned? That a life without meaning and purpose is a prison. A life where you are doing what you think you should do, what you must do, and what you need to do, is no fun. It is a life of obligation that leads you to regrets. Seriously, you only get one shot at this thing called life, so make it count.

I am, as we all are, created to be a blessing. We all can be a gift to others. Not just sometimes but always. But the challenges and difficulties of life weigh us down. The struggle and striving to have more stuff and status believing, "If I just get, fill in the blank, (______) it will all be okay." This is the lie the world advertises on an endless loop. A lie that happiness can be found in the satisfaction of having something outside of yourself. Let me make it clear and simple. If all the stuff and status mattered, you could take it with you when you died. And the No. 1 regret of the dying – they wish they dared to live a more authentic life. Not that they had acquired more status and material items.

Isn't it interesting how people who follow the dreams and desires of their hearts are much happier and more pleasant to be around? What delights your souls and excites you so completely that your brilliance inspires those closest to you? This, my friend, is your gift. This brings out the best in you, making life better for all involved. Everyone has a voice that can birth unlimited creative expression. Yes, that means you. You are beautifully and uniquely made to carve a path like no other, and that requires and demands you unleash your voice, that whisper of hope, love, and joy inside you to guide you. The voice that will speak what you seek until who you are meant to be is completely free.

My purpose, passion, and mission are to help as many people as possible experience joy and enthusiasm by discovering the unique, beautiful voice that resides inside them. In reading this, I hope to remind you that life is sometimes difficult and hard. Yet it is also wonderful and amazing. And for some, finding amazing is on the other side of hard. Do not give up on your dreams. There is no one like you, and there will never be another you. This world deserves to experience the blessing of You.

"We may encounter many defeats, but we must not be defeated."
Maya Angelou

DR. NICOLE BRADFORD

"Truly, I say to you, whoever says to this mountain, 'Be taken up and thrown into the sea,' and does not doubt in his heart, but believes that what he says will come to pass, it will be done for him."

(MARK 11:23, ESV)

When I Learned to Trust God

Growing up, life was tough for me. I was the youngest of six kids, born into a family of five girls and one boy. Being the youngest, I only grew up in the home with a sister five years older than me.

At times we were what I thought was a very normal family, and there were times when there was a lot of tension. I witnessed domestic violence, family members went to jail, and I had a tough time learning at times because I was not a super smart kid.

As I grew up, it was difficult for me because the siblings I wanted to accept me rejected me. I was told at times that I thought I was "white" because I talked differently and raised my kids differently.

The rejection from my siblings because I was the only child that went to college hurt. I just wanted them to see me as a sibling, and I just wanted to "fit in."

After living at home, I attended college and married my high school sweetheart. I thought I may have had tension during my childhood, but it had to get better with my in-laws. Well, that was a horrible assumption.

My in-laws rejected me because I was not who they wanted me to be. They had an image of who they wanted as their daughter-in-law. I would need to view marriage the same way they did.

I would need to have the ability to relate and connect with my husband the way they did in their marriage. I would need to fall in line when it came to how I raised my children and what holidays I would be allowed to have. When I first got married, I was told, "It was the four of us before you came, and it will be the four of us when you are gone."

Rejection is difficult to accept. Especially when all you want is to "fit in." It was always my thought that my in-laws were able to select who they loved, decide how they raised their kids, and choose where they went on their holidays; so why did they feel the need to control me and if I did not allow them to control me why "label" and then "reject me."

I never understood why it became a source of contention because how my husband and I decided to celebrate our birthdays because it was different. They did what they believed was right in their marriage. I never understood why it was wrong for my husband and me to spend time together and go to doctor appointments just because they chose not to in their marriage.

The rejection from my in-laws caused arguments within my marriage and, at times, planted seeds of doubt. They would say, "If Nicole loved you, she would xxx." If we made a decision and were ok with it, those words would resurface and negatively affect our marriage.

Yes, my in-laws' rejection caused several points of contention between my new husband and me. I then began to try and fit into the work world. I was taught if you work hard and do your best, you will be fine.

Whenever I worked, I would always give 110%. I wanted to "fit in," I wanted my supervisor and coworkers to like me, but that was not always the case. To "fit in," you cannot be different.

Of course, I have been different my entire life, and it has caused me to be rejected. If I worked and did not laugh at a certain joke, or if I was being mistreated my someone and I reported it, if I didn't just accept it and go alone, I would become the problem.

I was in search of acceptance from everyone around me, but why? Why did I need a group of people that did not love themselves to approve of me and who I was becoming?

I have spent a lot of time trying to figure that out until I truly began to trust God. My life, in my eyes, had been a mess, but despite that mess, God loved me. I would get angry at him from time to time because everyone that went along to get along seemed happy.

When I stopped trying to force my family to accept me as I am and stopped trying to convince my in-laws that I was a good person and get their acceptance and approval, then my life started to change.

When I began to stop trying to get my boss's approval at work by trying to "fit in," my life started to change. It began to go in a positive direction when I learned that God is my source and provider.

Things improved for me when I let go of the life that I thought would serve me and began walking, talking, and believing in God.

God is the source for everything, but until I stopped running from person to person seeking their approval, I always had a dim light because I tried to make someone who did not have light within them my source.

I always relate it to the outlet on the wall. When the lamp is not plugged into the outlet, it cannot shine brightly. I can try to plug the lamp into an extension cord, and it may work for a while, but the source begins to get weak.

Sometimes the extension cords may not be good and reject the lamp because it does not have space for three prongs. So, I had to remove my thought and opinion of everyone and everything else and fully depend on God.

Trusting in God means believing even when you do not see how it will work out. When I found my trust in God, I found my hope!

I found that people will support you today and be gone tomorrow. They may speak positively to your face, but it is another story as soon as you leave the room.

God, on the other hand, is consistent and will never leave your side. I understand that God has created me for a greater cause. Therefore, I must put aside my wants and desires and trust God and his plan.

I thought if I put aside who Nicole truly was and did what my family wanted, what my in-laws wanted, and what the people wanted on my job, I would be accepted, and then I would be ok.

As I learned to throw away my outline for my future, I heard God say, "Now live, Nicole! Live for me. Stop trying to please everyone else and place your faith and hope in me. I will provide you with everything you need."

The bible verses that keep me encouraged and the verses that allow me to trust God include:

If you were of the world, the world would love you as its own; but because you are not of the world, but I chose you out of the world; therefore, the world hates you. (John 15:19, ESV)

The fear of man lays a snare, but whoever trusts in the LORD is safe. (Proverbs 29:25, ESV)

For I know the plans I have for you, declares the Lord, plans for welfare and not for evil, to give you a future and a hope. (Jeremiah 29:11, ESV)

Trust in the Lord with all your heart and lean not unto your own understanding. (Proverbs 3:5, ESV)

In my 48 years on this earth, I have learned that it will get tough, I will get discouraged, and be rejected, but I must always trust God. It's when I trust in God that I find hope to continue moving forward!

KARENA CALHOUN

12 "For the word of God is living and active, sharper than any two-edged sword, piercing to the division of soul and of spirit, of joints and of marrow, and discerning the thoughts and intentions of the heart. 13 And no creature is hidden from his sight, but all are naked and exposed to the eyes of him to whom we must give account."

(HEBREWS 4:12-13, ESV)

I Want My Daddy!

My earliest childhood memory is of me saying, "I want my daddy!" as tears ran down my face during a traumatic event.

As I cried the words, 'I want my daddy!' I had no idea who my daddy was, and at that moment, it did not matter to me that I didn't know him. What mattered was that I had hope in someone I believed would come and protect me.

To my recollection, I had never met my daddy. I could not tell you what he looked like. I would not have recognized his aftershave or cologne. For that matter, I did not know if he had facial hair to shave or wore cologne. The truth was that I did not know anything about him except that I needed him. I needed someone's protection.

At that moment, my only thought was, whoever he was, I needed him right now, and I hoped he would show up soon.

Whoever he was, he did not show up. Any hope I had was lost. He would never know the tears that streamed down my face at five years old. He would never know the fear and trauma I felt and experienced during that time. He was nowhere to be found, at least not through my five-year-old hope-filled tears.

Years went by, and I still did not know if he wore cologne of any type. I knew little about him, not even what he looked like. I still did not know if he had facial hair. I did not know if he was tall, short, slim, or robust. I only knew his name.

I wandered through my formative years for the next four years, not feeling connected to anyone or anything. I felt abandoned and without an identity. I had no idea who I was nor WHOSE I was. I just seemed to exist. Hope was beyond deferred for me as far as I was concerned. Yes, even at such an early age, I was aware that I had hope that never seemed to materialize.

Around the age of nine, family members introduced me to lesbian sexual acts that no child should ever know. Any hope I had of trusting anyone, male or female, was dismantled at this point. Any hope of knowing who I was and how I should live my life was gone.

I never told a soul about this year-long assault that took place. Although there were adults who knew, nothing was done to protect me. So here I was at nine years old, already hollow on the inside.

As I continued to grow through life, it was in my teenage years that I began to realize I had no hope for the future. To be clear, I was not necessarily hopeless. I simply had no idea what hope was because I could not look to the future and see myself accomplishing great achievements.

So instead of being like most of my female counterparts who were dreaming of the ideal boyfriend who may turn into the perfect fiancé who may then turn into the ideal husband, my life went on. I turned inward ever so heavily to protect myself.

I remember thinking, "God, I hope this doesn't mean I'm gay." I have never been attracted to females, and everything that happened was not by permission. I was NINE YEARS OLD! They made me do it. Hope was lost as far as I was concerned.

As time passed, I became an adult whose childhood was lost and seemed to have been a blur in many instances. I imagine that I blocked out memories to maintain the sanity I had as a child.

Eventually, I had a baby girl of my own. As a single mom, I married a man who never asked me. He simply walked up to me one day and said, "I'm going to marry you."

From what I understand now, narcissists have an uncanny ability to pick out their victims. The soon-to-be victims have little to no hope of anything. He had me pegged. The emotional and, at times, physical abuse quickly zapped any hope that had been hiding in my soul.

This abuse went on for years. I could not understand what I had done to deserve it, and I couldn't figure out how to get out of the situation. Life for me at this point became more about numbing myself than anything. I began drinking.

In the beginning, it started so that I could wind down after work. Then it was drinking on the weekends. Then it became a daily routine.

At my final breaking point and an all-out abusive marriage, my daily routine looked a little like this; Wake up at 6 am. Drink a beer to calm the overnight withdrawal effects of shaking, nausea, and headache.

That one beer to calm my nerves is called the 'hair of the dog.' My hope each morning was that it would do it for me. It would help me cope throughout the day. That was where my hope lay.

After dropping my daughter off at school, I'd head off to work. After working 8 - 12 hours, I'd get off work, feed and take care of my baby girl, and then drink a six-pack of beer. That was just the beginning. Often, the six-pack became a 12-pack, and by the end, I was well into a case of beer a day. I'd do this day in and day out for several years.

One year, the cycle began to include a Tylenol PM pill at night to help me sleep. After a few of these incidents, I went to my doctor because I was groggy and could not fully wake up.

He immediately told me, "I can have you arrested for attempted suicide, and your daughter will be taken from you, or I can allow you to leave here and drive to the Psychiatric Emergency Room." I took the latter option. On the way, I stopped to get a drink.

I downed the beer in the parking lot of the Psych ER and went inside. I told them what they needed to hear to let me go and was on my way home within a few hours with another drink in the car.

After that, I stopped taking Tylenol PM but kept drinking. My doctor prescribed medications designed to prohibit the desire to drink alcohol. Unfortunately, I drank beer while taking the medication, so it had no positive effect on me.

When HOPE found me, I was doing my best to drown as many memories of my life as possible with alcohol. The day HOPE found me is the day alcohol left, the daddy issues left, the abandonment issues left, the depression left, the thoughts of suicide left, the memories of a sexual assault left, the emotional abuse left, and the physical abuse left.

The day hope found me; I cried, "I want my daddy and My Father in heaven," my Daddy, my Hope showed up.

I was 34 years old. I was tired of being abused by words, actions, and the deeds of others. I was tired of feeling sorry for myself. I was tired of drinking.

I woke up at 6 am to get ready for work. I was prepared to drink my 'hair of the dog.' Instead, I sat in bed as I heard a man on the tv say, "If you have tried everything, nothing has worked, and you want the love and peace of Jesus in your life, then repeat after me."

I knelt beside my bed, cupped my hands in prayer, and repeated those words with all I had in me. I didn't know this Jesus, but I knew I needed Him.

Today I realize the moment I did this at 34 years old at 6 am, about to take the hair of the dog so that I didn't go through withdrawals, was the same as five-year-old me crying, "I WANT MY DADDY." And this time, HE CAME.

I have not had a drink since that day. I experienced no withdrawals, and I have no alcohol-related health issues. I've learned to love, forgive, and live my authentic life. I'm no longer ashamed of who I am and who I thought I was.

I've since met my biological father - I'm thankful to God that I didn't know him. But that is a story for another book.

The last time I cried for my daddy, God in Heaven came. This was indeed the day HOPE found me.

AMY CHESS

"Come near to God, and he will
come near to you."

(JAMES 4:8, NIV)

My Passenger was Jesus

She was in the car, and the radio was blaring, as usual. She was upset, in the grip of panic. Her mind was spinning with so much clutter. At first, it was all just in her subconscious, but then she started to voice everything consuming her thoughts. Everyone and everything in her life was a mess. She was trying to be there for everyone, whether physically or mentally, and it was wearing her down. Nothing about her life was going smoothly. She felt like she was a puddle on the ground. Her strong and nurturing self had melted away and left a weary and weak person.

She reached over and turned off the radio. Complete silence. Something of a rarity, as music is such an important part of her world. The conversation with herself was heated. One hand was on the wheel, and the other was frantically gesturing. She was passionately expressing her thoughts out loud, mainly to the windshield in front of her. She finally had that last straw added to her back. She felt utterly broken.

This frantic scene went on for miles as she traveled down the highway. Passersby looked over at her as they noticed the lone woman driving the car, shouting to no one.

She needed to get a grip. Shouting and complaining about her situation was getting her nowhere. She was usually a positive person. She usually did not dwell on the negative. She tried to live by the advice given to her by her grandmother. Don't relive your problems over and over. "They happened to you once, honey. Why would you want to have them happen to you again?" She usually liked to move forward and find a solution. What was happening now?

She was out of her element. She decided to pray as she had never prayed before. She started by asking God for help. She offered up her prayers with tears streaming down her face. She was begging for God, for Jesus, to intervene in every area of her life. Every area needed rescuing. For miles and miles, she poured her heart out to God. Then, finally, she began to grow calm and took deep breaths. The prayers started to turn into a genuine conversation. She calmly shared what was unraveling in her world, her concerns, and her worries. Her breathing calmed, and she began to think rationally as the miles rolled on.

Suddenly, Jesus appeared in the passenger seat. It was not a shock. He never said a word. He was a calming presence, nodding with a gentle smile. She kept driving and talking. It was as if it were the most natural thing in the world; to have Jesus in the car on the way to work. She would look over occasionally to see his reaction to what she was voicing. It was as if she were chatting to a dear friend who never interrupted and let her thoughts spill out into the open so she could clear her head and then contemplate what she had just said. It was magical.

She grew increasingly calm as she continued voicing her thoughts. As she traveled down the highway, she finally began to feel hope. Her desperate situation seemed somehow lighter. She began to feel peaceful. She felt she could manage things with time, patience, and Jesus.

At that very moment, Jesus disappeared. It was as undefinable as when He arrived. She did not mind that He was gone. She kept talking as if He were still there; because she knew He was and would always be with her.

Yes, that was me. I often think back to this journey, the most incredible experience of my life. I have told very few people. It felt so personal and special. However, now I see that so many other people can benefit from hearing about my amazing ride. People need to hear this kind of hope. Our world is hurting, people are reliving their woes and troubles repeatedly, and they grow weary from being continually broken.

But those who hope in the Lord will renew their strength. They will soar on wings like eagles; they will run and not grow weary; they will walk and not be faint. Isaiah 40:31 (NIV)

I am not promising that you will have the same experience I had. However, I know I feel closer to our Lord than ever in my life since that day. I have faith that He is always with me. I know firsthand that I do not need to see Him to feel His presence to believe.

May Our Lord Jesus bless you and your life.

CORINNE COPPOLA

"We wait in HOPE for the Lord; He is our help and our shield. In Him our hearts rejoice, for we trust in his holy name. May your unfailing love be with us, Lord. Even as we put our hope in you."

(PSALM 33:20-22, NIV)

The Moment

You've had it!

Once you become a certain age, you have had THE MOMENT—the moment when life is altered forever, in good and not-so-good ways.

This story is about a devastating moment that became my life's biggest gift. It is the moment where there was a life BEFORE and a life AFTER. To the outside world, it was invisible, but to me, at this moment, time had stopped.

Looking back, it was the moment when I became real. Not in the sense that my life had been unreal but in the sense that my life became authentic, gritty, and unbearably difficult.

In late May 2007, memories surfaced of childhood sexual abuse by a close family member.

I was dazed, confused, overwhelmed, and in shock. My entire world had shattered. My family was my life. The shame, embarrassment, confusion, and rage permeated every cell in my body.

THE MOMENT began an unraveling of my life for which I was unprepared and certainly ill-equipped. At that moment, little did I know that it would be "the first day of the rest of my life." That moment launched a path of awakening that I could never have planned for.

When I spoke my truth to a few chosen family members, I was rejected and thought of as a liar. Ties were severed with my family and close family friends. Relationships ended, and I was beyond devastated. I became an orphan by choice.

My best friend rejected me, and my husband was contemplating leaving the marriage within a month. People who had committed their unconditional love and acceptance to me were gone; I felt unmoored, as if there was no safety net. I was beyond devastated. I was untethered and thought I was on the edge of a nervous breakdown. I was utterly lost and felt terrified, alone, and isolated. At the time, there were few opportunities for support, as sexual abuse and suppressed memories were not part of public conversation.

I had no idea where to begin to find help. I had never heard of someone suppressing memories for almost 40 years, especially with something like sexual abuse. I was desperate for answers and help; I felt abandoned; I was an outcast, and I thought I was losing my mind. I was hardly functioning and needed a way to show up for my three young children and my life. It felt as if I was living in a dream or a nightmare. It had to be someone else's life. I had sunk as low as I had ever been.

And this is when Hope Found Me.

Through Grace, I found help through a nature-based weekend retreat for women survivors of sexual violence and counseling through a local non-profit. These two events helped put me on a path of healing, recovery, strength, and resilience I never thought possible. They saved my life. I was able to bring these secrets out of the dark and into the light. I was seen, believed, and given a voice so the road to healing could begin.

As I realized and accepted what had happened, I began a journey of self-discovery. For most of my life, I had a short fuse, acute rage, distrust, and uneasiness around men. For many years, I attributed this to the physical and emotional abuse I experienced as a child. Then, I realized it was much deeper than that – I started to understand everything more profoundly. The unspeakable had happened to me, and I was determined to heal – for me, my children, and my children's children.

At the time of the memories of sexual abuse, I felt annihilated. I did not see the gift in the situation at all. I only saw betrayal, deceit, dishonesty, and lies. The wounds were deep, and I thought I would never be able to recover or regain a sense of myself. I was filled with loss, grief, rage, shame, disbelief - overall emotional and spiritual devastation.

And it was amid all of this I never lost faith. Instead, I found the strength to persevere. I chose to go on, heal, live another day, and somehow create good out of the unthinkable. I was broken, frozen, and traumatized; today, I am strong, resilient, thriving, and free. I am rewriting my family story through my children - living in truth, trust, authenticity, and love. I began a legacy of healing in my family that will affect many generations.

I have dedicated my life to serving and helping others overcome obstacles. I work with ordinary, everyday people who feel stuck or overwhelmed, and I help to shift their mindset and reclaim a life of authenticity, ease, and joy. As a result, I have been able to transform this tragedy into one of the greatest gifts of my life.

Kintsukuroi ("golden mend") is the Japanese art of repairing broken pottery with gold or silver. The mended cracks become part of the object's design, and the pottery is thought to be more precious and beautiful by going through the process of being broken and repaired.

There were many times that I felt hopeless, worthless, confused, demeaned, and broken beyond repair. But somehow, I had the inner resolve to continue – I was determined not to let what happened to me reflect who I was in this world. I focused on my continued healing and strength to feel my way out of hell. The truth must be told, and issues must be brought to light.

"The cracks are where the light has been let in." - Leonard Cohen

Most importantly, I have learned that God keeps His promises.

Although I had been physically sober for several years, I did not have emotional sobriety. I had to learn how to regulate my emotions in a healthier manner. I decided to work the twelve steps differently and saw God's promises come alive in my life. It was true what they say about 12-Step recovery; it is a program of spiritual awakening.

I realized I was powerless over others, and my life had become unmanageable. As I worked through the program, relationships were restored, my business started to thrive, and God has put me in places with people I could not have imagined (this book being one of them). I started to do 2-Way Prayer practice and began to have an intimacy with God I had never experienced before - He became my Papa, and I stepped into my place as one of His beloved daughters.

As for my ability to move on, it simply came down to the choice to always choose another day; even if I did not get out of bed, and the pain felt like shards of glass in my chest, I was determined to come out of it whole and healed.

Although I would never wish my experiences on my worst enemy, I am grateful beyond words for them as they have shaped me to be the person I was meant to be in this world – a healer, a teacher, a mentor, and a connector.

And so it is, as I step into my power and speak my truth. "Today is the first day of the rest of my life."

EMMA DAVIS

"An overwhelming feeling of calm radiated over me as I awaited an uncertain fate in the hospital."

A Beautiful Accident

On a warm August morning, I was deep in the wilderness leading a multiple-day horse camping experience. My guests wanted to see a horse gallop, so I hopped on our lead mare bareback. I effortlessly floated above her powerful stride as she charged down the trail—until she bucked and screeched to a halt. I flew over her head and under her legs. I can still see her droopy lip, round belly, and thundering hooves as they trampled me into the dirt. I lay on the trail, trying not to leave the world black. My boyfriend, of only two weeks, grabbed my degloved hand to keep me awake — it worked. Max didn't tell me my spine was sticking out as he radioed for an airlift. An hour later, the phrase "music to my ears" made sense as I heard the helicopter buzzing over the mountains.

An overwhelming feeling of calm radiated over me as I awaited an uncertain fate in the hospital. My first-ever surgery was going to be at least eight hours long. I woke up feeling as heavy and stuck as a cinder block on the ocean floor. Someone I had never met fused my spine across five vertebrae. It was unclear if I would walk or go to the bathroom on my own. When I asked if I could ride a horse again, I was asked, "Why would you want to?" They didn't get it.

At twenty-one years old, my life was heading in an unexpected direction, but it was the best thing to have ever happened to me—it showed me who I am and what I'm capable of.

I moved home so my family could take care of me. They sponge-bathed me, wiped my butt, and forced protein shakes down me as I watched my muscles atrophy and wither away as I lay in bed for months. I should have been paralyzed from the waist down, but I wasn't. Thanks to CrossFit, my abdominal muscles held my spine in place just enough to not sever my spinal cord. Yet I had to endure a year-long recovery that started with learning how to roll over. The nerve pain took my breath away and forced uncontrollable tears down my cheeks. Despite the pain, I was so thankful to feel my legs. I wasn't going to throw away my second chance.

Two months before the accident, I adopted a wild mustang, Mikko, from the United States Government. I was to train Mikko for the ranch where I worked. At the time of my accident, I could barely touch his nose. His innate sense of self-preservation was strong. He was flighty and sensitive, it was going to take time to gentle him gently, and even then, he probably would not have been a good fit for the ranch. The ranch sold him without telling me. No one knew where he went after that. I spent many hours in bed staring at the walls wondering where he was. I needed to get back to horses—they were my driving force.

Physical therapy was literally and figuratively slow going. I went through the small motions knowing they would lead to larger ones but stepping off a curb wrong was always a humbling experience. Nevertheless, I was happy to be stepping at all—especially after being told that was all I would be able to do.

Max had sat with me under the hot summer sun, awaiting the helicopter, and again a week later in the hospital—both times, he tried to hide tears from me. In those moments, I knew we were more than a summer fling. We spent the next two years long distance. He celebrated all the small and large victories of recovery with me. When he visited, he helped me into my body brace and held my hand as I gingerly took calculated steps. It was an interesting way to start a relationship but incredibly telling of who a person is. When I told him I wanted to ride a horse again, he kept his reservations to himself—perhaps he also knew he couldn't stop me.

To ride a horse again, I needed to build my body back, piece by piece. When I returned to CrossFit, I felt like the wind could blow me over. Holding two pounds felt like two hundred. A retired Orthopedic surgeon turned coach brought me back to life. "Doc," as I call him, donated his time and expertise to help me. He pushed me when I was unsure, and slowly I began to push him. Then, one day, he stepped out to get coffee, and I snuck in my first pull-ups. When he returned, he knew something momentous had happened. I didn't say a word and showed him. He may not admit it, but there was a tear in his eye. At that moment, we became friends for life. I owe a lot of my recovery to him.

As soon as the doctors declared me "healed," I found myself atop a black horse. As his steps shifted us side to side, I felt pulls in my back but continued. I missed floating above the ground.

I thought about Mikko. You don't forget someone you love. Never did I think he would randomly appear on Craigslist a year later. It was him.

I had to get to him. And when I did, he was thin, and his coat was dull as dirt. Fear ran through his face. As he rounded the corner, I stopped breathing. He locked onto me, and his small nervous steps turned to ground-covering, thundering strides. He placed his head on my chest. We had only known each other for two months and then separated for over two years.

I didn't know it, but he would become my greatest teacher. I'm not sure of what he endured, but I am sure it was horrendous. He clenched so hard that he shook uncontrollably at a light touch, which usually led to an explosion. His fears ran deep. I was told the kindest thing to do would be to euthanize him. I was also told never to get on him, especially given my back. The only thing I listened to was my gut. Among many things, my recovery instilled in me patience, dedication, and hope. All of which became amplified again in Mikko's presence. I hired people to help Mikko, but he tore their ligaments, burned their hands, and broke their bones.

No matter what, he was with me for life. We spent hours walking trails on foot, just the two of us, not asking a lot, just wandering from one patch of grass to the next—between some blowups, of course. Then, two years after we reunited and after trainers had tried and failed, he allowed me to ease onto his back. Bareback and with just a halter, we took our first steps as a mounted team. The metal in my spine held me tall and strong, reminding me of what's possible if you release expectations as you head toward a goal. Strange, I know.

If you came across Mikko and me on the trail today, he would probably veer over to say hello to you. You might remark about the large white freeze-brand on his neck, identifying him as a wild mustang. I'd tell you a bit about it—perhaps you didn't know wild mustangs are roaming across the United States, and if you didn't know that, then you certainly didn't know about the controversy surrounding them. You might pat him and thank us for stopping, but he mandated that we did. You would never know that not too long ago, he wouldn't dare approach a stranger. You would never know that I thank the universe every day for using my legs and being in that moment with you and him.

We would part ways. I'd pat Mikko on the neck as I smiled, recounting all we have been through and the endless possibilities that lie ahead on the literal and figurative trail we walk together. A trail filled with hope.

MICHAEL FURLONGER

"Now, this is eternal life: that they know you…"

(JOHN 17:3, NIV)

The Father I Never Knew

Before I get into my story for When Hope Found Me, I want to explain my title: The Father I Never Knew.

I have an earthly father. His name is Kevin Furlonger. He worked long hours in my childhood, teaching me, by his example, that a man is willing to work long and hard to be a provider for his family. It wasn't until my preteen years that my family and I moved closer to the city so we would be an hour closer to my father's business and have more time together.

From the age of six or seven, we were a church-going family. At six years old, I was hit by a car and nearly died from a brain injury. This incident may or may not have been a driving force behind my family's faith.

In the city, my father turned his local warehouse into a church after our church leadership split. My father would operate as a "lead" sound technician in several churches, as well as a leader at a Christian camp, and play a Roman guard in several Easter plays.

This isn't a dramatic story of an absent father and a son pining for a father's affection. Instead, this is the story of a church boy growing up in a carnal world who never knew the love of his Heavenly Father.

There are many different verses that I considered as my "token" verse. For example, I could have gone with Ecclesiastes 3:11 (NIV), which tells us that God set eternity in the human heart. Or I could also go with 1 John 2:19 (NIV), where John, addresses the people who left the faith community: They went out from us, (because) they never belonged to us.

The point of all this is to illustrate that I never knew God.

And, in a sense, I still don't.

How can anyone say that they know the infinite and eternal God of the universe? But I can say that I now better understand the gospel message of Jesus Christ.

I grew up believing God is this big meanie who wants to smite us for looking at Him wrong. But Jesus Christ steps in front of God with his lightning bolt and says, "NOOO! I'll take their place." And the Holy Spirit, well, He didn't come up much.

What made things more confusing? Grace. We're saved by grace through faith, so don't try to live a holy life because that's religion. Works do not save us. I was lost with no direction.

The Bible is full of rules we are now told are of the old covenant and thus ignored. And the wisdom of the New Testament, the new covenant, is ignored because of the payment of Jesus Christ's death on the cross for our sins.

And Jesus Christ's death on the cross clouded my understanding of a loving God who saw fit to sacrifice his only son. Is it any wonder I was confused?

So, if you can imagine, I'm a teenager going to church on Sundays, being an obnoxious Bible-thumper to people at school, but in private, I'm suicidal and looking at trash on the internet.

Now, this teenager who knew that sinning was wrong but did it anyway because, well, grace, grace, grace, right? This teenager grows up watching shows where sex is glorified and becomes a man. He has a job and a car, and he starts dating.

I will trust you to imagine the chaos that my life was becoming. I was still attending church, mind you.

The Word of God becoming less and less read from the pulpit, and the concrete truth of that Word being substituted for personal dreams and visions, rolling on the floor, and barking like a dog are all signs of God supposedly speaking to you.

And all I want is to believe that God hasn't forgotten me. And maybe God would put me where I might belong because sex became less about pleasure and more about belonging.

If the church doesn't invite me to their social groups, I will find somewhere I will be welcome.

One of the changing points in my life was when I said "No" to a girl. It may seem small, but my whole perception of who I was changed in that moment.

I didn't have to define my value by whether the church accepted me or whether I had these extra-biblical revelations from God. I knew that God disapproved of this sin I was contemplating.

Now, I wasn't growing spiritually at church. I was very alone. I continuously fought with myself about living a sinful lifestyle because that was the only place where I was welcome. But I knew it was wrong, not by a vision, but from the Word of God. So, I began to read and then write.

I wanted to know, "Why are certain things sinful?" And more importantly, "Why are the things that I would otherwise enjoy deemed sinful?"

I started writing my book, God: The Master of Sin and Satan the Beautiful.

The title may confuse you, but it's quite simple. God placed Adam and Eve in a garden where there is one tree of Knowledge of Good and Evil. Why did God plant such a tree if He didn't understand good and evil?

And Satan the Beautiful is simply about the character of Satan. He deceives. He makes sinfulness have an attractive appeal to it.

I started in Genesis 1:1 (NIV), "In the beginning God created the heavens and the earth." Then, I started reading and taking notes.

In the creation story, we have God in His great wisdom creating all things. In the fall, we have Satan deceiving mankind. Then we have the rules. And finally, the redemption.

We see God banishing man and woman from the garden, and I asked, "Why?" God is a God of forgiveness; surely, he can overlook these sins. But we read in Genesis 3:22 that God was concerned about the state of sinful man and potentially that sinful man taking from the Tree of Life and living forever.

As I was writing, I was going through the creation story, the flood, Sodom and Gomorrah, the Exodus story, and the laws, and the weight of every one of these sins was becoming more and more prevalent in my life.

I started reading for alternative ways to eternal life other than God. I know that seems silly. Why would anyone want eternity with God if you're trying so hard to avoid Him? I know I'm not the only person to try this.

For with much wisdom comes much sorrow; the more knowledge the more grief. Ecclesiastes 1:18 (NIV)

When I was given the topic, When Hope Found Me, I was reading a particular law God gave the Israelites. In Exodus 22:16-17 (NIV), "If a man seduces a virgin who is not pledged to be married and sleeps with her, he must pay the bride-price, and she shall be his wife. If her father absolutely refuses to give her to him, he must still pay the bride price for virgins."

I remember looking at my bank account and thinking, "I don't think I'll have enough to pay off my debt." I remember praying, "Lord Jesus, pay off my debt." And it was like a new understanding of the whole Bible hit me.

When Jesus died on that cross, my debt was paid.

A friend once asked me, "There is a law that says that if a child disobeys a parent, they are to stone the child. How can your loving God say such a thing?"

They did not understand God's law. God's requirement of absolute holiness is so steep that no man, woman, politician, or athlete will ever be able to make it to God. The Old Testament laws and sacrifices were to illustrate for us all the magnitude of our sins and the weight they carry.

Now, I don't know when salvation happens; whether I was saved when I prayed the "sinner's prayer" (which isn't in the Bible) at six years old. Or whether I was saved at 26 years old when I began praying on my knees that God might destroy my soul to spare me the punishment I am due. Or at 30, when I recognized the beauty of God's holiness and holy law and aimed to live for such perfection.

But I do know that I am saved because of my Heavenly Father's love for me. And, with that, I have hope.

D.C. GOMEZ

Blessings From Strangers

Mass shootings, homicides, war, and just plain terror - that's what bombards us every day. Our news outlets have become centers of sensationalized commentaries, each trying to outdo the other. We are on sensory overload, and we are often only expecting the worst.

As a writer and motivational speaker, I'm seen as a super-positive person. But even the most optimistic person can have a moment of weakness. I faced one of those situations not too long ago. Where the influence of the media filled me with terror, but the goodness of humanity prevailed.

The sun was blaring down on Interstate 22 as I drove back home to Texas from Savannah. It had been a long week at the convention but an absolute blast. A quick stop for gas and food marked the halfway point back to Texas. According to the GPS, I had seven hours left (if I didn't stop) before I made it home. For a person who hates driving, this was a painful situation. My only ray of hope was that I would arrive in Texas during the daytime. Many people don't know I suffer from PTSD attacks while driving at night. It's one of the few times I have flashbacks of my convoys in Iraq.

After the lunch was secure in the car, a trip to the bathroom completed, and a check-in text sent, I was ready for the road. Reggaeton was playing on the radio, my frozen cherry coke was neatly placed in the cup holder, and I had a smile on my face. It had been a glorious week, and I was back on I-22 for the next half of my road-trip.

Then it happened. A thunderstorm rolled in. While many areas of Texas were suffering droughts, the luscious green hills of Alabama were living their best lives. Rain poured like the heavens themselves had opened the floodgates. I reduced my speed, held the steering wheel with both hands, and focused on the road. The worst of the storm was behind me, or so I thought, before the 2020 Honda sedan I rented hit a patch of water. Like one of those scary movies, the vehicle hydroplaned to the right.

My life didn't flash before my eyes. That would have been epic. Instead, I lost control of the vehicle and slid down the side of the embankment. I would like to tell you, my friend, that I was brave or even stoic. That didn't happen. As the car went down, I closed my eyes and screamed like a child. I didn't want to see it coming if this was the way I would go. Saint Peter could give me the details of my ending.

The roller coaster ride from hell didn't last long, maybe forty-five seconds. The bottom of the embankment stopped the ride, triggering the airbags to engage. The impact of the airbag hitting my face forced my eyes to open. The car was smoking. That fabulous drink I ordered earlier was now covering my pants and shirt. Panic set in as the emergency navigation started talking about the accident that had occurred. Like I didn't know I was in an accident. I stuttered, trying to make sense of my situation.

The extremely pleasant attendant called 911 and asked me if I could exit the vehicle. Like a miracle from God, the door opened. I was two feet off the ground, and not sure how on earth that car didn't flip over. It was perfectly horizontal, suspended on the V-shape of the embankment. Grass and trees were all around me, and shock wanted to take over. A man maneuvered his way down the hill to help.

Thankfully, he was a doctor and in full control of his thinking capabilities. He asked me to turn the vehicle off, which stopped the smoke. Taking deep breaths, I found myself struggling to stand up straight. My back was killing me, and I couldn't find a comfortable position to stand. The rain slowed down, but not enough to avoid soaking me.

In less than seven minutes, the first responders arrived, and the doctor took his leave. I never did learn his name.

I was stuck in an embankment between an Interstate and a Highway, giving the jurisdiction to Alabama State Troopers. Blessings came, but at the time, I didn't see them. How could I? I was soaking wet, hurt, and terrified. To add to my horrible situation, I looked like a wet cat after a terrible thunderstorm. My shirt had stains from the cherry coke that I had never tasted.

My self-defense mechanism kicked in, and I started cracking jokes. I couldn't help it. It's my first reaction to danger. I've been doing it all my life, including my time in combat as a soldier in Iraq. It made everyone wonder if I was hurt. The tears hadn't started, but the shock was strong. My world crumbled as they strapped me to the ambulance gurney, my only possession that of my pristine-looking purse. I was even mad at my purse. Why did nothing happen to the damn thing? Not even a drop of the red drink.

Pieces of reality started floating into my brain. I was being transported to a local hospital. The rental, which was now totaled, would be towed away. To where? No idea. My girl at the rental place was going to kill me. The battery on my phone read less than twenty percent. I was stranded in the middle of Alabama on a Sunday with no way to get home. Every horrible Hollywood movie charged my brain. Was this a new version of "Get Out" or one of those Stephen King books? This was not the best time to be a writer with a wild imagination.

The ride to the hospital was short. The wait, on the other hand, was endless. My back hurt like all hell, but the fear was even worse. After I recounted the accident for the fifth time and my vitals were taken, I broke down. In between nurse visits, the tears took over. Pain and fear plagued everything I did. I called home, and the more I detailed the occurrence, the more afraid I became. My best friend panicked. My parents were in terror.

It took me hours to calm down. My fight-or-flight response would not release its hold on me. Around six pm, a shift happened. Maybe it was me, or maybe the universe had come to my aid, but angels came to my rescue left and right. The hospital staff realized I was stranded in another state. While transportation in this small town was unavailable (no cabs, Uber, no Lyft, no nothing), the officer in the hospital gave me a ride to the closest hotel. A passing stranger in the hospital allowed me to use his charger since no one else had one.

My arrival confused the receptionist at the hotel. But like a saint, she gave me a toothbrush and toothpaste. The empty room was overwhelming. I was safe, but with no way to get home. My parents contacted my brothers to calm me down. The blessings of brothers, they would not let you fail. Both of my brothers went on standby for their own "rescue mission to Alabama." Whether it meant one would fly from California to get me or the other drove the seven hours from Texas, they didn't care. They would get me home.

For the first time in twelve hours, I wasn't alone. I just needed to make a call. The next day, filled with beautiful sunshine, I started making calls. Getting out of the small town was harder than I imagined, but the people were amazing. I got hugs from strangers, offers to drive me anywhere I needed for a rental. At the end, the towing company (whom I had never met) picked me up and drove me an hour away to the nearest airport for a rental. They never asked for a single thing except to make sure I was okay. My girl at the rental place, who is now one of my biggest heroes, moved mountains to get me a vehicle.

On Sunday, I wondered, "Why me, God?" Why was I stuck in the middle of nowhere?

On Monday afternoon, with two compressed fractured vertebrae, bruises all over, with all my possessions and over a dozen people cheering for me, I asked, "Why me?" again. What had I done to deserve these many blessings?

The world is a beautiful creation. Water on the road might take us out for a while. But the power of human compassion will always find us in the most unlikely places. Today, I am grateful for the blessings of strangers.

ERIN HARRIGAN

"Abide in me, and I in you. As the branch cannot bear fruit by itself unless it abides in the vine, neither can you, unless you abide in me. I am the vine; you are the branches. Whoever abides in me and I in him, he it is that bears much fruit, for apart from me you can do nothing."

(JOHN 15:4-5, ESV)

I Could Only Look Up

Ever find yourself face down on the Berber carpet crying out to God from what you think is rock bottom, asking, "How the hell did I get here?"

If you have, you are surely not alone, and those of us who've had that experience come to it from many different situations. Some from trauma, abuse, or addiction. Others from self-reliance, pride, and an insatiable need for achievement and recognition.

No matter the situation, when you find yourself in that position, with chest tightening, shallow breath, and guttural sobs, you pray for a way out. You pray that someone - what you think may be God or some higher power - can hear you. And that they will save you.

Save you from the situation. Or even save you from yourself.

I found myself in this face-down position, soaking my Berber carpet in tears, in 2014.

Let me take you back a bit.

I'm the oldest child of four, raised by a single mom in the suburbs of Washington, DC. While we, fortunately, had a roof over our heads, we still lived hand-to-mouth, shopping at the local food pantry and wearing hand-me-downs. This mainly resulted from my parent's divorce when I was 11, which left my mother working multiple jobs to make ends meet since my father's child support was non-existent.

That pre-teen season is tenuous, without the extra layer of unkempt hair and mismatched clothes. Those things might have been cute for my younger siblings (7, 5, and 3 at the time), but not for an almost-teenager. I could feel the eyes looking down on me and hear the snide remarks about me at school and in the neighborhood. I could hear my mother's whispered (and sometimes heated) conversations with her twin sister (from whose sons the hand-me-downs came) and my grandmother about how we were surviving. And what I saw clearly in my head full of dreams was I needed to do big things to be a big deal, earn big money, and get the heck out of Dodge.

I suppose that started my quest as an achievement-chaser. I wanted people to see me as far more than my clothing, hair, and messy face appeared. This powerful desire for recognition and approval built my tenacity, perseverance, and drive, propelling me through high school, college, and the corporate world. It was the classic recipe for building an overachiever. It served me well as I climbed the corporate ladder, found an equally hard-working husband, and started a family—all on my way to building the American dream that had bypassed my childhood.

At each milestone, I forged ahead, seeking greater accomplishments, and taking all the credit for my hard work. A six-figure salary, big title, big house filled with all the name brand furnishings, luxury car, etc. At each level, I praised God and prayed for more.

Yet, each level was never enough. I still felt empty.

When corporate life outpaced quality family time, I decided the only route to the time freedom and greater wealth our family "needed" had to be entrepreneurship. So, I found a network marketing venture that took my tenacity and drive to a new level, and I successfully straddled both the employee and entrepreneur worlds (overachiever, remember?). Again, I praised God for the success and prayed for more. When my corporate job downsized me, I praised God for His grand plan - now I was free to build my own business and live that dream life I had been planning!

In 2014, two years after the corporate downsizing, I was all about the hustle. Driving and striving to replace the income we had lost. While my business was doing okay, it only brought in two-thirds of my previous income. Yet we were spending as if we never lost a dime. It felt like running in place. I was working harder than ever, yet my business was stagnant. I was praying hard, but it seemed like God wasn't listening. I was invoking all the new age, the law of attraction techniques I could (thanks to having soaked up knowledge from The Secret, yet never having read the Bible), and still nothing.

Clearly, disaster was looming.

It was a humid day in the fall of 2014 when I was face down on the floor, crying out for help. We were behind on our mortgage, racking up debt, and we had drained my 401K. All in the interest of living out this dream life. All built on my pride for being a successful "mompreneur," "boss babe," etc. From that dark hole I had dug, I could only look up.

I reached out to a mentor in my business for help. This amazing woman would remind you of the graceful Audrey Hepburn. She was soft-spoken yet firm and always willing to tell it like it is. I like to think of her as a velvet hammer. She listened intently, then firmly and lovingly said: "Erin, I don't think you know who you are or whose you are. Do you have a relationship with Jesus?"

There it was. That 5-letter name I'd been avoiding all this time, thinking Jesus was a mashup of new age philosophy, the universe, and this figurehead. I'd been praying to God, circling my desires in prayer (keyword: my), and getting myself tangled up on my way to the top. And that question was like the road-closed sign in my path. It stopped me in my tracks and left me wondering, "Do I actually know Jesus?"

The answer was no.

And in my darkness, a light shined.

That day, October 4, 2014, hope found me. A place from which I could only look up and raise my hands like a toddler saying, "Up. Up!" to its mother. That day I decided that I would no longer worship my business as an idol, and it would no longer be my savior. Only Jesus deserves that role.

And giving Him my life changed everything.

No longer did I have to drive and strive to prove my worth. No longer was my identity tied to reaching the latest achievement I was chasing.

That day, He made me brand new.

The way I viewed life and business changed. The way I did business changed.

Was it perfect? Definitely not. Are there stops and starts? Absolutely. Did business suddenly explode? Not at all.

But He took over as if to say, "Why don't you rest and let me drive for a while?"

And I did (well, mostly).

During this time, a foundational verse emerged for my life and business journey:

Abide in me, and I in you. As the branch cannot bear fruit by itself unless it abides in the vine, neither can you, unless you abide in me. I am the vine; you are the branches. Whoever abides in me and I in him, he it is that bears much fruit, for apart from me you can do nothing. John 15:4-5 (ESV)

Without Him, we don't even exist. Without Him, we are never fully nourished. It is only in the abiding - aligned with, enmeshed in, submitted to - that we have a full life, full nourishment, and produce fruit that matters. Fruit that changes the world. He is our portion and our source. In Him, we have all we need.

Today I help other ambitious women of faith to realize His business strategy is best and help them to tune out the world, tune into His truth and turn up their focus. And this enables them to walk out His assignment with clarity, serenity, and fulfillment.

Those were the things I truly sought my whole life - clarity, serenity, and fulfillment. Yet I was looking for them in the roles (daughter, wife, mom), the work (corporate executive, entrepreneur), and the outcomes (money, house, car, name brands). I was looking for love (purpose, fulfillment, success) in all the wrong places, as the classic song says (thank you, Johnny Lee).

But in the darkest place, hope found me. And He can find you too!

JOANN HARRIS

"For I know the plans that I have for you, declares the Lord, plans for prosperity and not for disaster, to give you a future and a hope."

(JEREMIAH 29:11, NASB)

Hope in the True Source

Have you ever hoped for something that you felt was yours, but the situation did not turn out how you thought it would? Have you hoped for something that seemed so far-fetched that you knew you needed divine intervention for it to happen? Have you ever felt you did not want to get your hopes up because you fear disappointment? If you answered yes to any of these questions, I trust that reading a bit of my story will encourage you, ensuring that when you hope, you hope in God.

For some time now, I have felt there is more to do in this life regarding my vocation. There seems to be something that has not yet been fulfilled by working a 9 to 5 job alone. I am grateful for where I am planted in this season of my life. However, I know God has placed so much more on the inside of me that has yet to be realized. So, I have embarked upon a personal development journey over the past year. And what a journey it has been.

A little over a year ago, I was introduced to a personal development program that was of interest. I sat through the 3-day live online sessions, learning much along the way. At the end of the last day, an offer was presented for a next-level program. I heard the needed financial investment, going back and forth in my mind regarding what I would do because the offer on the table was for a limited time. So, I took the next step, speaking with a customer service representative, who encouraged me to take the leap and make the financial investment. I felt that the avenue I hoped for to further my development and growth was here, yet, at that moment, I was not experiencing complete peace about signing up. Therefore, I did not accept the offer, looking at what seemed to be, the opportunity of a lifetime, leaving the dock and sailing away into the sunset without me onboard.

For some time, I hoped for an opportunity like this, which seemed perfect. Thoughts of me hoping for things in the past that did not work out began to creep up in my mind. Wait, I now have some new tools I gained in the 3-day training; therefore, I shifted my mind, focusing on how to apply what I learned. Perhaps what I hoped for (participating in a formalized personal development program) did happen, just not how I thought it would. Maybe it was not about the next level program but me learning what I will need for my journey in the completed sessions.

A few months later, I was introduced to a similar 5-day program. Almost immediately, negative thoughts started coming to mind regarding the last program I thought I was to pursue. But I told myself, "I will push through and remain open to new opportunities." So, I signed up for the program, filled with excitement and apprehension, still hoping, and looking forward to what could be.

Each night, we had an assignment to complete and submit. Two winners would be announced each morning, receiving a voucher, which could be used toward one of the next-level programs. The winners' names would be announced, while profile pictures would be shown on the screen. I began to feel a bit nervous because of my past experiences with hoping and being disappointed. Then a scripture I had read many times came to mind:

"Why art thou cast down, O my soul? and why art thou disquieted within me? Hope thou in God: for I shall yet praise him, who is the health of my countenance, and my God." Psalm 42:11 (KJV)

What stood out to me was the part of the scripture that said, "Hope thou in God," which I spoke aloud repeatedly.

I was determined to complete each assignment nightly, knowing that out of 500 plus program participants, I could only be considered for the prize if I submitted the work. What I did differently this time was intentionally place my hope in God, trusting Him to work things out His way. On Day two, the winners' names were called; however, my name was not one of them. On Days three and four, again, my name was not called.

Yes, I began to waver a bit, but I checked myself and prepared to work on the assignment due that evening. As I prepared to get started on the assignment, something extraordinary happened. I experienced a divine download, hearing what to do and seeing what the final product would look like. I gathered the supplies needed, excitedly working to completion. When ready to submit my assignment, I asked my husband to take a picture of me with the final product, submitting it before the 11:59 p.m. deadline.

When logging in the next morning for the last day of the live training, I had butterflies in my stomach, yet I could hear the scripture ringing softly in my ear, "Hope thou in God." Since this was the last training day, the sponsor selected three winners. When it was time to call the names, I heard the first person's name. It was not mine. The second person's name was called, and I heard congratulations, Joann Harris. What? When I looked at the computer screen, I saw my picture and name. I cried and called out to my husband, who was in the next room, "I won. I won. Hope thou in God. I won." Oh, what joy filled my heart and my day. The voucher I won was enough to cover the next level program I desired, which I successfully completed a few months later.

For years, I have engaged in what I call misplaced hope. Incorrectly placing my hope in people and situations, focusing on the wrong source from which to draw hope. I hoped that people would come through. I hoped that things would happen, causing all the pieces to fall in line. I hoped that someone's answer to my request would be yes. Until then, I trusted temporal resources instead of the eternal source. The God of the universe who is sovereign and always has my best at heart.

To be honest, many things I hoped for were neither His best for me nor my best. I often compromised, knowing that some relationships and opportunities were not for me. However, I allowed the temporary pain of being alone or meeting the expectations of others to drive my decisions to hope for what was never to be mine in the first place.

As a result, I experienced the tug of war between what I desired (guised in sincere hope) and what I knew deep down within to be the truth. When situations did not work according to my plan, I would take on a victim mentality, shedding a few tears and sinking deeper and deeper into the negative self-talk that kept me tethered to unfruitful living. And when I hoped for something that I did not desire, and it happened, I would portray happiness, putting on the mask of contentment while feeling a sense of emptiness and internal uneasiness.

When placing hope in God, I was reminded that He is not a genie in a lamp, expecting Him to do things in my time and way. Instead, I am learning to bring what I desire to Him while being open to His yes, no, or wait. The key is that while I hope, I make room for His sovereignty. As I hope, I emphasize Him, looking forward to how He will work things out for my betterment.

I collided with true hope on the day I decided to hope in God, allowing hope to find me at the right place. This is the kind of hope that causes me to hold on no matter what, the hope that knows that the best in life awaits me, the hope that all is well even when it does not look or feel like it. Though I do not always understand why He does what He does, I believe in Him and trust He knows what is best for me.

TRACY LOWRY

"Now faith is the substance of things hoped for, the evidence of things not seen."

(HEBREWS 11:1 KJV)

But What If I Don't Have Hope?

A few years ago, I was standing with my high school graduation class, listening to the choir sing the well-known song, "I Hope You Dance." If I could sing well, maybe I would have rewritten the song and sung it to you. But since I don't have a singing voice, I will write instead.

As I look back on my life, it is full of mountain peaks and riverbend valleys. Winding roads, twists and turns, highs and lows, hopes, and despairs. So, when asked to participate in this fabulous collaboration, I sat in front of a blank computer screen with a blinking vertical line. I had no idea what I was about to write.

When did Hope find me? What was that pivotal moment? Was it some monumental event? Was it the morning after a hellacious night? When was it? After weeks of contemplating what I was going to say, I realized I would write this a little differently than I have written so many other pieces in my life.

It may sound ambiguous, but Hope can be found in so many ways. I can't think of one shining moment where Hope found me. It never left me, and still, I hold on to it forever more. Maybe I'm strange that way. But I'd like to think my experience could help others who may find hope in the same fashion.

Hope, to me, is something that can come and go. We don't always have Hope, but we sometimes need to find it or even work for it.

Hope is not the absence of doubt but the belief that better things can happen, even when there are no current signs for them to happen.

I feel, and I must admit the idea is not completely original, that there is a scale of emotions, from the bottom of the barrel to the highest of highs. Hope, to me, can be more in the middle of the scale. You may feel depressed, lonely, sad, abandoned, and downright crummy. But even in those times, I have found Hope. Hope that things can get better. Hope that things will turn around. Hope that tomorrow can bring a whole new set of opportunities and growth.

Now, this could start to sound like I don't regard "hope" as a very elevated feeling or emotion. This is not the case! I believe we must learn to walk before we can run. We need to be able to add and subtract before we can do algebra. Likewise, we need Hope to change the trajectory of our situation in life. Without Hope for a better outcome, there is seldom an action made to make those changes happen.

Without Hope, I would never have gotten pregnant after multiple miscarriages. Without Hope, I would never have applied for the job I thought was "out of my league" and then thrived at it. Without Hope, there would be no improvement or change for the better, getting out of addiction, finding new jobs, new relationships, new dreams, or a life worth living.

Fear is a powerful thing, but Hope can be stronger. Hope doesn't have to start large but can appear in small baby steps. You can hope that tomorrow will be a better day. You can hope that you will find a job that pays the bills. Then when you find that, you can hope that the job of your dreams is within reach.

Some definitions feel too constricting. The truth is there can be many degrees of Hope. You can have a little bit of Hope, or you can have a lot of Hope, and everything in between.

Is a lot of hope ideal? Sure! But if all you can do is muster up a little bit of Hope, then hold on to it tightly and never let it go! This has a snowball effect. You can start with a small snowball and roll it around in the snow to make a huge snowman. Then it can build and grow.

You still must put in the effort to push the little packed snowball around. Of course, the bigger it gets, the harder it gets to push around. But also, the bigger it gets, the more visible it is. Something great can be made with it.

So, what if you don't feel you have any hope? I know I don't know you personally. But I have been in your shoes and will make a bold prediction. You saw this book for a reason. Call it fate, call it God, call it the universe, but you saw it for a reason. You choosing to pick this book up and read the words I'm typing right now shows me you have at least a glimmer of Hope for something better.

Pat yourself on the back and give yourself some credit. You are already a step closer than you may think. You at least have a glimmer of Hope. You have a tiny snowball that you can now work with. Now it's time to build that small snowball into a snowman or whatever it is you want to make out of that small bit of hope.

Building on Hope takes some self-discipline, I'm not going to lie. But, if you are like many of us in the world, you want to say, "Great! I found some hope! Now I want a huge snowman family with kids and grandkids. Oh, and I want it all RIGHT NOW." (I may be talking of myself here, bear with me.) But to build your faith and Hope, it is important to start small.

When addicts begin the journey of becoming sober, we must learn that they celebrate ALL the milestones! Start with one full day sober. Celebrate that! Now you know you can do it for a day. You were able to stay sober for a month. Celebrate that too. It may sound too simple to celebrate to some people. But they may not be your people.

Then you hit six months sober, one year, and your confidence grows with each day, week, month, and year. Is it easy? No, but nothing worth doing is.

Our Hope can do the same thing. We already established you have at least a glimmer of Hope, or you wouldn't be reading this book right now. So, hold on and let it GROW! I believe that Hope is the starting point for ANY accomplishment or situation. Will you fail? Sometimes. But Hope is what helps you get back up to try again. Only now, you try again with experience. You have learned what to do and what not to do.

The choice is yours. You have a glimmer of Hope. Are you going to help it grow and get bigger? Or will you let that light die out, along with your life, Hope, and dreams? I love the song "I Hope You Dance." Dancing is great; however, I want to sing "I Hope You Hope." I hope you hold onto that Hope and continue to foster it into something great! It can make great things happen.

Are you going to hope in people who have let you down? Yep. Hope anyway.

Are you going to be disappointed at times? Yep. Hope anyway.

Are you going to gain a life worth living if you hope? Yep!

The choice is yours. And I HOPE YOU HOPE!

BETTY PREDMORE

"I lift my eyes to the hills. From where does my help come? My help comes from the Lord, who made heaven and earth."

(PSALM 1221: 1-2, ESV)

Hope Found in the Hills

It is often hard to find hope in our deepest moments of despair, but our God never fails us, even in the darkest of times. He meets us where we are and knows exactly how to bring light back into our hearts.

The phone call came shortly after 6:00 a.m. My dad experienced an "episode" in the wee hours of the morning, and I needed to get there quickly.

I made the two-hour drive to the hospital in far less time than I should have, as fear gripped me in a way I had never experienced before. My mind knew that my heart wasn't ready, and this day would change my life forever.

I walked into a room filled with doctors-in-training who were listening to the actual doctor explain my dad's situation. At first, I was upset by the crowd until I remembered that we were in a teaching hospital.

He lay there, attached to machines, unable to speak, and looking so terribly frail. At that moment, fear was pushed further into my heart as an enormous feeling of hopelessness invaded every fiber of who I was.

The nurse gave me a sympathetic pat on my arm as the doctor explained that my dad could not breathe on his own. Lung cancer had finally caught him, and there was no way out of this pit of despair that was swallowing me.

I knew what had to happen. We had many talks about this exact moment, and his wishes were very clear.

There was nothing my heart wanted to say less than giving permission to disconnect him. That was the hardest moment of my life to date, but I refused to disrespect his wishes even though every part of me wanted to keep him there.

I looked into those faded eyes that had sparkled with mischief so many times in my life and said, "I love you, Dad." "I love you too," was his whispered reply.

My mind flashed to all the millions of moments we had shared over the past four years since I had become his caregiver. Moving him into my home was one of the greatest blessings of my life.

There is no gratitude, no words of thanks, that I could offer up that would describe the blessing of those last years with him. The cups of coffee on the porch, the laughter at his crazy stories, the times he listened while I vented my latest frustrations, our secrets, our lunch dates, and milkshake excursions.

And there were those sweet moments when he would take a grandchild by the hand and sneak a treat to them, pull money from his wallet, and send them chasing after the ice cream truck, or sit on the swing and tell them stories.

Those who previously knew him would likely say, "Who is this stranger, and what have you done with the real Jazzbo?" But the truth is, that was the real Jazzbo (my father's nickname in the writing community), a man who loved his children and grandchildren and enjoyed his last years peacefully being catered to by one and all.

My memories flew even further back to the five-year-old girl sitting in front of her daddy on his motorcycle and screaming, "Faster, Daddy, faster!" And to the time when I was fifteen, and he showed up at the apartment complex pool in his Speedo, which caused me to want to hide in the deep end.

There is something so surreal about looking at a person who has always been larger-than-life in your mind and seeing them so fragile. This brilliant man whose words were read by so many would have no more words to type, no more words to entertain the mass of followers he'd acquired.

With his son on one side and his daughter on the other, the machines were turned off. My thoughtful sister-in-law placed her phone on his pillow as Softly & Tenderly played in his ear.

I was hopeless to fix this; hopeless to do anything but be by his side. And to the words "All who are weary, come home," he took one last breath in one of the most peaceful moments I have ever experienced.

To watch your father, take his last breath, is both torture and blessing at the same time. I pray that as I struggle through, the Lord never lets me forget the peace of that moment. I pray that I never forget his eyes looking into mine as he said, "I love you."

With my heart broken into a thousand pieces, I sat with him for a while, not wanting to walk out that door for the final time. How do you leave someone lying there and just walk away?

I did finally leave to make the long drive home. The rain falling around me matched the tears falling from my eyes and the dread I felt in knowing I had to go home and tell some little children that their granddaddy would not be coming home.

My heart was so heavy, my burden so immense, I couldn't catch my breath. So, I prayed and asked God to give me the strength to endure this and walk through it with the dignity my father deserved.

I felt the presence of God in the car with me, and I leaned into His strength, letting it penetrate through me. I was not alone, and God would give me exactly what I needed to get through this loss.

God spoke to me in that moment, driving through the mountains of Southern California. He reminded me that I could also find some joy in my sorrow and hope in my most hopeless moments. My dad had accepted Christ into his heart a few years prior, after a colorful life that was fodder for many stories. Because of this, I could have the beautiful hope of reuniting with him in Heaven.

So we do not lose heart. Though our outer self is wasting away, our inner self is being renewed daily. This light momentary affliction is preparing for us an eternal weight of glory beyond all comparison as we look not to the things that are seen but to the unseen. The things that are seen are transient, but the things that are unseen are eternal. 2 Corinthians 4:16-18 (ESV)

My dad's earthly body may have come to an end, but each day he had been growing stronger in his spirit. The cancer was horrible, but his reward was eternity with God in a place of peace and joy, with no pain to be found.

This hope offered me something to hold on to as I walked the journey of grief, a long journey for me. It has been my reassuring promise of a beautiful reunion day.

I have had so many moments when the sorrow of this loss has threatened to overtake my entire heart, but I have been able to cling to the hope that found me in the hills that day. It has been the life raft that has kept me afloat in my most turbulent waters.

For that, I am forever grateful to the God of hope who has never left my side.

SANDRA POTTORF

"And the God of all grace, who called you to his eternal glory in Christ, after you have suffered a little while, will himself restore you and make you strong, firm, and steadfast."

(1 PETER 5:10, NIV)

Restoration of Our Quilted Life

Today as I was examining timeworn clothing for a sewing project, I imagined what my quilt would look like. As I placed the bulky bag of my choices into the craft closet, my arm brushed up against two cowboy shirts hanging there. With a slight jump of my heartbeat and a little catch in my breath, I quickly recognized these familiar items - shirts that I had given to my husband so many years ago when we were dating. A few days ago, he had cleaned out his closet for things to donate, and these two shirts were among the rejects. I rescued those shirts and stashed them away, still immensely drawn to the many memories.

Twenty-some years ago, the shift at my part-time job was over for the night. I was sitting at the bar with my boss, lamenting about the revolving-door life I had been having with short-lived relationships. He asked me if I ever wanted to be married again, and I hesitantly replied, "maybe...someday." He answered that I deserved a good man that would treat me right. A few bar stools away, someone was listening -- a man that I later learned had decided that HE was going to be THAT man!

Soon after, a friend from the bar handed me a napkin with a dinner invitation and phone number. A customer trusted her to give it to me. I remember that I was most impressed that each word was spelled correctly and the handwriting neat. Even the grammar was correct. I decided this man was worth at least one dinner!

We soon became a couple, engaged, and married within the year, embarking on a second marriage for both of us. Many complicated issues needed to be worked out; we both had children and financial obligations that made the budget very skinny. We also decided we wanted to attend the church where we had been married.

When my husband lost the one job he had worked for years, I was livid, angry, and unable to cope very well. Several drastic changes came about in a short time. He attended a recovery program as an outpatient; I took a new position with more responsibility and money. It took months before he found new employment with a modest paycheck.

His alcohol usage was still evident as we worked through things the best we could. I thought it would change like a miracle cure after he completed the recovery program. At that time, I didn't grasp that alcoholism is a disease that is, at the very least, a difficult addiction to overcome.

We were invited to attend a Christian program for those with any kind of addiction. In the beginning, I went to be supportive of my spouse. He was the one with the problem, not me. I wanted to know how to fix his problem. This program was very revealing about addiction. I quickly found myself humbled by the blatant truth that nothing I ever did or said would stop his addiction. I had to learn to focus on my recovery for control and anger issues. And let him work on himself.

We stopped going to that group after a couple of years. My husband was unable to work due to his medical condition. Our relationship suffered as we continued working on separate issues while staying together. I worked full-time and had a Christian counselor, support group, and endearing friends that helped me remember that I was valued.

After a powerful worship service one Sunday, my husband went to the altar. The Pastor prayed for total deliverance from his addiction. He truly seemed to be seeking help this time. I had prayed so many times for God to heal him; many times, in tears, giving up my desire to control our marriage and promising to get out of God's way.

One evening I came home after work and found my husband on the floor where he had fallen and could not get up by himself. The EMTs with the local ambulance service lifted him into his bed several times that weekend; he refused transport for medical evaluation each time.

A couple of days later, he fell again with the bathroom towel bar broken in his hand. He asked for the ambulance this time, aware that he might not come home soon.

He left in the ambulance, and I collapsed on my couch, overtaken by what had just transpired. In no hurry to get to the hospital, I absorbed the precious silence around me as strength to prepare for this new reality. Then, finally, I heard my voice thanking God for whatever he had planned for us now.

The ER doctor said his condition was very serious; that he might live a couple of months. His liver had failed, and his body was very yellow. We called our Pastor to come and pray with us.

When we were alone, we finally talked as if for the first time in months. We prayed together that God would carry us through this storm. I accepted that God would take him soon and end his suffering; that had been my prayer for quite a while.

A few days later, I heard one of the doctors cheerfully tell my husband that his "numbers were up." He was doing better but still had a long way to go.

My silent implosion went surprisingly unnoticed. I wanted to scream out that the doctor had to be mistaken. He was supposed to be dying! I was prepared for his death, waiting for it to be validated. But instead, I left the hospital so angry that I could not make sense of it. And for a few hours, I was confused, pacing my living room, yelling at the sky, and crying so hard.

How could I share this with anyone? I would be considered a heartless lunatic. The guilt I was holding was proof of just that. I reached out to a confidante that listened to me rant. She metaphorically stuck a pin in my bubble of pain as she explained that I had processed what I assumed was happening and accepted it. I had to process it all over again, which I was stubbornly defying.

The next day an odd thing happened. A dead cat was on the highway right in front of our house. It bothered me that this beautiful cat had been left unclaimed for two days. I felt obligated to rescue the carcass from the road and give her a proper burial. The thought that this pretty baby may have been someone's pet, or she may not have been loved or living a life of warmth, infuriated me. As I kicked the shovel into the dirt with my boot, I sobbed with no restraint. I had expected someone or something to die. I was angry it did not happen.

After four months, my husband came home. It occurred to me that God had separated our broken lives to allow us to heal from our own mess and come together again each time. Neither one of us knew what to expect.

And the God of all grace, who called you to his eternal glory in Christ, after you have suffered a little while, will himself restore you and make you strong, firm, and steadfast. 1 Peter 5:10 (NIV)

As I looked at those old shirts again, a huge wave of love swept over me, bubbling to the surface from where I had restrained it for a long time. My husband and I continue to rebuild the trust between us. We are worth it. As of this writing, in 2022, he has reached one year of sobriety.

We do not know where we would be without the HOPE God always provides for us; HOPE is woven into every strand and fiber of our lives. We must learn which knots are worth untying and which need to stay intact.

God has given us that HOPE. The realization that we can believe and have faith in what we cannot see. We can know beyond all earthly comprehension that there is always Hope with our unchangeable God, the Hope that is found only in a right relationship with Jesus Christ our Lord!

RITA PRESTON

"But for you who revere my name, the sun of righteousness will rise with healing in its rays. And you will go out and frolic like well-fed calves."

(MALACHI 4:2, NIV)

Disorder's Burdensome Path

The rheumatologist spoke one word: Fibromyalgia. I was certain he was wrong. Until three or four weeks prior, the thought of another chronic illness had been the farthest thing from my mind. (I am a lifelong asthmatic.)

I hurt. All. The. Time. My entire body. Every joint. Every muscle. Every nerve. Some days only a couple of spots. On other days, my pain level was well over ten on the 0-10 scale. Discomfort engulfed me from my scalp to my toenails, not missing a shred of organic matter in between.

Pre-Diagnosis.

My family doctor prescribed arthritis medication. Finally, I informed her it was not helping. She referred me to a pain management center.

The first course of action at the pain clinic was a regimen of three prescriptions "to get the pain under control." My sister, an RN (Registered Nurse), was horrified when she heard the drug combination, terrified that I was going to work every day and driving. According to her, that combination should have knocked out an elephant!

Funny, it did not phase me. It was like drinking a glass of water. Sis worried that the cocktail of three did not affect my faculties. I assured her it had been that way since Day One. I reminded her that our mother had taken serious meds for spinal pain and remained cognizant, saying it was just like drinking water. Apparently, Mom and I shared a high resistance and tolerance to medications.

Over the next couple of years, my meds were adjusted. Eventually, I weaned myself off them since they were making no difference. I was 'treated' to a couple of spinal injections in the lumbar region and the cervical area (neck) – not a procedure for the faint of heart! In addition, I had hip and shoulder injections. Mostly the results were the same, like drinking a glass of water. No relief.

Diagnosis.

Finally, I was referred to a rheumatologist. He examined me and administered the pressure point test. I had never heard of pressure points. All but one or two of the eighteen designated spots reacted! Doc ordered a myriad of tests, from lab work to bone density. He had to rule out all other possibilities to confirm a fibromyalgia diagnosis.

Less than a month later, Hubby and I made the long trek to the rheumatologist's office for review. Remarkably, the RA (rheumatoid arthritis that haunted me since age 5) did not appear in any results. Peculiar! That was good news, combined with confirmation of Fibromyalgia. The rheumatologist confirmed I was right to eliminate the pain meds since they were of little use in Fibro treatment.

Post-diagnosis.

Over the next few days, we shared the news with close family. My big brother's eyes got wet. I told him not to feel bad and that this would not kill me. He quietly pointed out that it could debilitate me. I hurt for him. I pointed out that I have grandchildren with whom to play, a Harley (Harley-DavidsonTM) to ride, and a life to live.

My brother had a point. So, I dove into research on my new companion, the Fibro-Beast.

Doctors gave me stern words to pace myself. WHAT?

I either ran full-tilt or not at all. For me, there was no such thing as pacing, except when watching harness racing at the horse track or pacing while talking on the phone. Could that qualify as exercise? I did not want to hear about pacing daily activities. Budgeting my time and not overdoing activity on good days. That is comical if you know me.

Typical for those with Fibro. We get a good day (a day when we do not feel exhausted like usual and are not having high pain throughout all body parts) and know we must make the best of it, so we flash forward like a freight train. Then, feeling exuberant, we plan our next day's adventures only to discover the next morning that we feel like we had been run over by a MackTM truck and want to sleep for a week.

It may take days or weeks to recover from that one good day. Still, we drag ourselves out of bed and off to work or the sofa. Those nearby will say how great we look or look a little tired. A little? We are sitting on the precipice of complete exhaustion and physical collapse.

We think back to yesterday and all that we did. We were glorious! We felt like our old selves! Today, Fibro-Beast laughs in our faces, ushering stinging tears to our faces. We second-guess ourselves. If we just had not tried to fit so much into yesterday. If we had just let a few things go. If this. If that.

Deep down, we know. We know it would have made no real difference. The enveloping fatigue. The flickering pain like the devil's breath. It returns with a vengeance.

Once you have a Fibro diagnosis, you begin to comprehend your past.

When I had a tooth extracted, and my bite shifted rapidly, maxillofacial pain ensued, yielding six weeks of physical therapy with a liquid diet and the good word that I needed braces. Eventually, I surrendered and signed up for 18 months of constructive torture. I remember relief as the pain faded away! Several years later, I read up on Fibro-Beast symptoms, one of which is maxillofacial pain. Coincidence?

In the past few years, the scientific community has chattered about a blood test called FM/a, detecting levels of cytokines and chemokines as indicators of Fibro. The University of Illinois College of Medicine Chicago conducted the ground-breaking research. I look forward to the day when this lab test becomes a gold standard of diagnosis! The FM/a is now covered by many insurance plans and is considered 99% accurate. So, there is hope for a smoother diagnosis!

As a fibro sufferer, I have been on the receiving end of barbs directed to bait me into defending the very pain I feel. It seems unreal that some people refuse to acknowledge a diagnosis of this disorder and try to tell us that we imagine our symptoms.

It is not a disease, virus, or ailment. It is a disorder, and the pain is real. Unfortunately, some people pretend we imagine the pain. Some people criticize us. I pray they never experience the myriad of symptoms a fibro sufferer endures.

What causes fibromyalgia? Anything, including but not limited to trauma (physical or mental), infection, and genetics, can all be considered sources. Considering humankind has launched people into space and brought them home safely but cannot cure a common cold, I am not surprised that we do not have a better-defined precursor or treatment for the Fibro-Beast.

Did I mention the diverse symptoms: poor sleep patterns, irritable bowel syndrome, pain, mood disorders, restless leg syndrome, and more? Unique to each patient, some symptoms are prominent, while others may be absent.

I do not want my words to echo a 'poor me' essay but, rather, an 'I understand from whence you come.' And 'I understand your pain' and 'Don't give up on yourself' affirmations. If the Fibro-Beast has invaded your life, know that you are not alone.

You do not have to let the beast win. Just consider it like a pager from your employer; you never know when the pain (pager) will alarm you. You CAN handle this. Surround yourself with those who will support you!

There is no reason you cannot climb this mountain! "39 He went in and said to them, "Why all this commotion and wailing? The child is not dead but asleep." 40 But they laughed at him. After he put them all out, he took the child's father and mother and the disciples who were with him and went in where the child was. 41 He took her by the hand and said to her, "Talitha koum!" (Which means "Little girl, I say to you, get up!"). 42 Immediately the girl stood up and began to walk around (she was twelve years old). At this they were completely astonished." Mark 5:39-42 (NIV)

With faith, anything is possible. Jesus could awaken the sleeping and the dead. So, too, can He keep me alive, lifting me to share His words. I will not succumb!

I continue my attempts at pacing. I am reminded, "Honest scales and balances belong to the Lord; all the weights in the bag are of his making." Proverbs 16:11 (NIV)

I shall carry this burden and, like the apostle Paul, cling to my Lord with gratitude and complete hope in his goodness to me.

ARLYN SMITH

"Spread love everywhere you go. Let no one ever come to you
without leaving happier."

MOTHER TERESA

I Was Doing All I Could to Die

I was only 23 years old.

I did not feel Hope in any aspect of my life. Since 15, my life was a parade of drug, alcohol, and eating disorder rehabilitations, hospitals, psychiatric hospitals, and institutions. Ambulances, overdoses, ICUs, incarcerations, life support, suicide attempts, ERs, anorexia, self-mutilation, police blotters, etc.

No one knew. I was a star athlete and student with long blonde hair. I lived in a gated community, went to a posh private school, and my father was a dentist.

The shame of being this way was so intense that I could not bear telling anyone how sick I was. Yet, people like me are "supposed" to have it all. People would say, "You have nothing to complain about," and question why someone like me would wind up as I did at age 23.

In a coma, on life support, teetering between life and death at 23, after another suicide attempt. The shame and stigma about who you are is so severe that you would choose death over the admission of a problem. Something is wrong.

There came the point where I was in a wheelchair, unable to move or speak. I often cried and thought, "I am now complete trash." I could not even attempt suicide again because I was unable to move. Otherwise, I would have.

Fast forward to 2013, and it hit me smack in the forehead. I AM ABOUT TO DIE. I don't want to die, but I will if I don't change. I will only get out of life what I give.

I finally understood that seeing only the bad had turned me into a cog in the hamster wheel of society. Hateful sensationalism sells. Chasing the Joneses. Believing the grass is always greener somewhere else.

When I was young, I thought everything was a war. Life was a battle. It was me against the world, erroneously believing that hate would always triumph. I then thought, "Hold the phone! I HATE "HATE!"

Hate has almost killed me. Judgment and intolerance have almost killed me. Yet I was doing the same to the world. When I pointed a finger at others, I still had three pointing back in my direction.

My hateful thinking had molded me into a statistic. One of those members of society who believes their problems entitle them to hate. Incorrectly surmising I was the only person in the history of existence to have challenges in my life.

I also did not understand at the time that my attempts to earn degrees, awards, and a big name was destroying me. I believed these things were the pinnacle of humanity. I put people with great achievements on pedestals and did not know how hard they worked to get there, thinking that somehow my parents simply "got us there."

I did not understand that my mother somehow raised three hyperactive children simultaneously. Took us to extra-curricular activities. Somehow remained calm while I barraged her with the most intense insults imaginable. I pummeled her with my anger at not correctly spraying my Aussie Scrunch Spray on my mall bangs or spewing bitter words to my father, who worked himself to exhaustion from morning to night.

Due to their demanding work, I went from taking my first steps on the balcony of a dingy TDY motel to a country club neighborhood and expensive private school, going from creamed tuna with peas and military bases to fine china and an indoor pool. For some reason, I thought we were poor. I am serious. I believed that my father was a lowly dentist, and my mother was some mere house fairy who never did anything with her life.

I made this abundantly clear to my parents. The fact that my family still loves me speaks to their character, not mine. I had reached a point where I believed myself to be a greasy, crumpled fast food bag full of chicken nugget crumbs at the bottom of a back-alley dumpster.

I needed help. I still do. I used to believe my admission of my problems would lessen me. I believed I had to give up if I acknowledged and accepted my alcoholism and eating disorder. I had to give up on everything, my hopes, and dreams. That admission of my problems would cause me to have a tattoo on my forehead. The world would need to be warned that I was "one of those bad people."

I am an alcoholic; this is not up for debate. The stark contrast between my sober life and my life bound by the chains of active substance abuse is not debatable either. Yet becoming increasingly optimistic has changed my life. I am acknowledging all the good in the world and focusing on it. I am not an unaware Pollyana who denies that bad exists; I choose not to entertain all the thoughts of the bad in the world.

Once I genuinely internalized that I needed help, I was free. To become all I dreamt for myself. The knowledge that I did not have to impress or prove anything to anyone was freeing. I had misinterpreted the idea of taking care of myself and my own needs as being selfish. For many reasons, I thought I had to be willing to destroy myself for humanity.

Once I realized how untrue my thoughts had been, I was off like a bat out of hell. Unencumbered by the past albatross around my neck, I was free to fly. All my dreams, before I fell into my addictions, came rushing back at warp speed.

I acknowledged that nothing in my life was a waste, and everything I went through taught me a lesson. I wonder what would have happened if I had ignored those lessons. I believe I would still be blaming others and not taking responsibility for my life.

Here is an example of how my life has changed. In 2019 following a routine MRI, my neurologist diagnosed me with ataxia, which is poor muscle control that causes clumsy involuntary movements. Upon receiving that news, I grinned and thought, "Well, I have to work harder now!" Things like this don't seem so severe when you have walked through hell your entire life.

In September 2022: I earned two gold medals at a USAPL Virginia meet for powerlifting in the open divisions. Not athletes with disabilities. I was competing against everyone.

As I gripped the barbell, I shut my eyes. Everything I had been through in my life swirled through my mind. My parents and fiancé were there. Everyone was on pins and needles. And I remembered how you receive what you give in life. I looked up and thought, "GO!"

I did it! Everyone cheered like crazy. I realized the entire world had been cheering all along.

I thought, "Arlyn, see what you can do when you cheer for yourself and the world?" I could hardly wait to thank everyone who inspired me with their own lives.

I plan to keep going, to keep moving forward, clinging to Hope. Hope for a brighter future; hope that God will continue to work in my life; hope that I will become the woman I was meant to be.

COREE SULLIVAN

"For I know the plans I have for you," declares the Lord, "plans to prosper you and not to harm you, plans to give you hope and a future."

(JEREMIAH 29:11, NIV)

Seriously, 3:00 am?

It was 3:00 am, and I was snuggled up, asleep in bed. Sleep was elusive at this time in my life, so I wanted to enjoy it when I was getting good sleep. Then, suddenly, my eyes opened wide. I knew something exciting was about to happen!

The date was September 12, 2012. I had been praying and crying out for clarity since January of that year about what I would do with all the pain and hurt I had experienced.

Here I was, divorced. Again. My business closed in 2009 due to the 2008 – 2009 economic crash. I had short-sold my home and lost my five investment homes to either short sale or foreclosure because of the financial debacle. And, to stay afloat, I had spent all my retirement funds trying to avoid bankruptcy but ended up filing anyway.

Not only was I at the end of my rope emotionally, but I was also financially broke. There seemed to be no hope for my future, and I slipped into a depression filled with hopelessness and despair.

Here I was, divorced three times with all the brokenness that comes with it. I was beginning to realize I needed to find a path out of my downward emotional spiral. Depression was heavy. I worked through the day but could not find peace at night. Things just rolled around in my head, I lost my appetite, and my thoughts were unhealthy.

My finances were a mess. I was struggling to pay rent and buy groceries. I had started a new job, but some weeks it did not pay enough to cover basic living expenses. As a result, I found myself going deeper and deeper into depression.

Pride kept me from talking to anyone about how I was feeling. I felt so alone. I had several friends and family members struggling, and I certainly did not want to burden them with my problems. If anything, I wanted to be their sounding board and help where I could. But at the end of the day, it was all I could do to keep myself out of the depth's depression.

Three years before this happened, I had gone through a divorce, moved back to my home state of Colorado, and began attending a Holy Spirit-filled church with my daughters and their families. I was happy to live near my family again to watch my grandchildren grow up. Inside, my heart had been so deeply broken. It was beginning to take a toll in every area of my life.

Attending services and special events at this church was my saving grace. I felt a peace there that I could not find anywhere else. One day I heard about an inner healing ministry called Sozo that was beginning at this church. I wrote down the information and made an appointment with the Pastor to learn more. At this point, I would try anything!

The Pastor set an appointment with two ladies on his team. It took two 3-hour sessions to get through all the pain and wounds that had built up in my heart from as early as four years of age.

In these sessions, I remembered that my mother had developed postpartum depression after my youngest brother was born. The doctors put her on the equivalent of uppers to boost her mood. When she could not sleep because she was so wound up, they prescribed downers to help her sleep. And when she got to the point that she was either high or down and depressed, they gave her what I call 'tweeners' to help her manage through the day on a more even keel.

This up-and-down cycle went on for a couple of years until, one day, she had a complete breakdown and ended up in the hospital. My maternal grandparents came to our house to take care of things as often as they could, but my grandfather became ill about six months after my mom's breakdown, so they could no longer help.

My mom spent more time in hospitals and mental institutions than out. So, at the age of eight, I became the lady of the house. I did the cooking, cleaning, and laundry after school and on the weekends.

When I was 16, my mom filed for divorce, and my dad got custody of my brothers and me. My household chores continued. My dad was a wonderful dad and a hard worker. We lived on a farm, so there was always something that needed to be done.

Dad made sure we went to church every Sunday and had a special lunch somewhere after church. Sometimes we would go for burgers after Sunday night church services instead because there was work to be done on the farm during daylight. But he always tried to make things as balanced as possible, given the situation.

Soon after their divorce was final, my dad met and began dating a woman that initially was the answer to my prayers. Of course, I wanted a mom that would do the things moms do, like cleaning, cooking, running my brothers to football practice, etc. But I also wanted to know about hair, makeup and how to dress in style like the other girls at school.

Initially, she was that 'mom' I so desperately wanted. However, shortly after she and my dad were married, everything changed. She became abusive and controlling. She manipulated my dad into doing things her way rather than finding a way to compromise with how we had done them for the past decade. As a result, I couldn't do anything right or please her. The wrath she poured out on my brothers and me was extremely hurtful.

We found ourselves wondering why our dad no longer protected us. Why did he allow her to be so abusive to us? We could not understand. For me, it went deeper because I craved a mom's nurturing in my life.

All of this came rushing into my memory through inner healing sessions. I found I had buried it all a long time ago. Plus, I had not learned that God was a loving God, not a god of rules, and if you didn't follow them, there were painful consequences to pay. At age 18, I decided I could never live up to those rules, nor could I make Him happy. So, I decided I would live my life and be as good a person as possible and quit going to church.

I married a man soon after high school that said he loved me and would take care of me for the rest of my life. That sounded like music to my ears since I had battled through my life from an early age. Eight months later, we were married.

I have learned that two broken people coming together is not a good foundation for a healthy marriage. We both had brokenness we had stuffed down deep, thinking that was how life was and marriage would make it better. But it didn't. We had two amazing daughters but divorced after ten years of marriage.

All this and more came to the forefront in my inner healing sessions. Things I had forgotten and things I remembered. It all was messy and painful but needed to be released to the One who designed me, Father God, so I could find the true healing I needed.

Hope found me in those Sozo sessions! Finally, the old had been healed and washed away, and I had a new beginning to start the rest of my life.

I adopted the scripture, "For I know the plans I have for you," declares the Lord, "plans to prosper you and not to harm you, plans to give you hope and a future." Jeremiah 29:11 of the NIV translation is my mantra. It still is to this day.

That 3:00 am wake-up call came a few days after my sessions. I had been asking God what this was all for. All this pain, the divorces, all this loss. In an audible voice, I heard Father God say, "I want you to war against the ravages of divorce."

God gave me the curriculum to use in a Divorce Recovery program I started shortly after that at my church. This information led me to write my book, "Destiny After Divorce," and God has used the book to bring hope to thousands of others, including the guidance He brings me daily. Through Him, there is always hope!

CONCLUSION

Did one of the stories resonate with you?

Each co-author, including myself, hope you finish reading this book and feel a spark of hope—a spark that begins or one that builds bigger.

As we travel along this road called life, we will inevitably face hardship. Each hardship is unique to the person and situation. How we deal with that hardship is where the hard work lies.

No one wants to feel hopeless, but if you do, remember that many people have gone through difficulties and come out of the other side—more than likely, stronger than before.

Look at it this way. You are still here. You are still living. That means you have a 100% success rate of making it through the tough days! You may be a bit battered and weary, but you made it!

Hope has a way of helping you to see the possibility of a better day.

I'll leave you with a few powerful quotes and hope your day has been made brighter by spending time with the pages of this book.

"Hope is the thing with feathers that perches in the soul and sings the tune without the words and never stops at all."

– EMILY DICKINSON

"We have always held to the hope, the belief, the conviction that there is a better life, a better world, beyond the horizon."

– FRANKLIN D. ROOSEVELT

" It's always something to know you've done the most you could. But don't leave off hoping, or it's of no use doing anything. Hope, hope to the last."

– CHARLES DICKENS

Thank you for reading this book!

Did you enjoy this book? Please leave a review. Reviews are so helpful for authors as they may help new readers want to pick up a copy and get their own dose of Hope.

Other ways to help get the word out:

- Share a link to the book or mention it on social media
- Pick up another copy to share with someone
- Recommend this book

www.kimlenglingauthor.com

Other books by Kim Lengling
Available on Amazon

Listening

To Your Voice Publishing
Annette Ruth Pearson

Email: info@ltyvpublishing.co.uk

Website: www.listeningtoyourvoice.co.uk

Publisher and writing coaching services

LinkedIn: https://www.linkedin.com/in/ruthpearsonltyv/

Facebook: https://www.facebook.com/Listening-To-You-Voice-Publishing

Instagram: @empoweringtransformations

"Let's toss nuggets of hope into the world like confetti."

Email: contact@kimlengingauthor.com

Website: www.kimlenglingauthor.com

Amazon Author Page:

https://www.amazon.com/Kim-Lengling/e/B00L9N6VBO

Let Fear Bounce Podcast:

https://anchor.fm/kim-lengling1

Let Fear Bounce FB Page:

https://www.facebook.com/letfearbouncepodcast

The Write Stuff TV Show FB Page:

https://www.facebook.com/TheWriteStuffTVShow